THE COMPLETE GUIDE TO CAVALIER KING CHARLES SPANIELS

Jordan Honeycutt

Publication Data

Jordan Honeycutt

The Complete Guide to Cavalier King Charles Spaniels ---- First edition.

Summary: "Successfully raising a Cavalier King Charles Spaniel dog from puppy to old age" --- Provided by publisher.

ISBN: 978-1-70885-6-052

[1. Cavalier King Charles Spaniels --- Non-Fiction] I. Title.

This book has been written with the published intent to provide accurate and author-itative information in regard to the subject matter included. While every reasonable pre-caution has been taken in preparation of this book the author and publisher expressly dis-claim responsibility for any errors, omissions, or adverse effects arising from the use or application of the information contained inside. The techniques and suggestions are to be used at the reader's discretion and are not to be considered a substitute for professional veterinary care. If you suspect a medical problem with your dog, consult your veterinarian.

Design by Sorin Rădulescu

First paperback edition, 2019

TABLE OF CONTENTS

CHAPTER 1

Breed History **10**
What Is a Cavalier King Charles Spaniel? **10**
History of the Cavalier **11**
Physical Characteristics **15**
Typical Breed Behavior **16**
Is the Cavalier the Right Breed for You? **18**
Cost of Ownership **19**

CHAPTER 2

Choosing Your Cavalier **20**
Buying vs. Adopting **20**
Importance of Breeder Reputation **21**
Finding the Right Breeder **22**
    Can I visit the breeding facility? **23**
    How long have you been breeding Cavaliers? **23**
    What genetic conditions do you test for before breeding and what
    conditions do you screen the puppies for before selling? **23**
    Can I see veterinary records for both parents? **24**
What kind of guarantee do you provide for your puppies? **25**
    Do you ever sell to a broker or pet shop? **25**
Picking the Perfect Puppy **28**
Tips for Adopting a Cavalier **29**

CHAPTER 3

Preparing for Your Cavalier **30**
Preparing Children and Other Pets **30**
Puppy-Proofing Your Home **33**
Dangerous Things Your Dog Might Eat **36**
Supplies to Purchase Before You Bring Your Cavalier Home **37**
Preparing an Outdoor Space **41**

CHAPTER 4

Bringing Home Your Cavalier 42
Picking Up Your Cavalier 43
The Ride Home 43
The First Night 45
Choosing the Right Veterinarian 47
The First Vet Visit 48

CHAPTER 5

Being a Puppy Parent 50
Have Realistic Expectations 51
Chewing 52
Digging 53
Barking and Growling 54
Separation Anxiety 55
Crate Training Basics 56
Leaving Your Dog Home Alone 59

CHAPTER 6

Potty Training Your Cavalier 60
Potty Training Methodology 60
Using the Crate for Potty Training 62
    Charles Weidig – BlackFire Cavaliers on Crate Training 63
The First Few Weeks 64
How to Handle Accidents 65
Pros and Cons of Doggy Doors 65

CHAPTER 7

Socializing Your Cavalier 68
Importance of Socialization 69
Behavior Around Other Dogs 70
Safe Ways to Socialize 71
Socializing Adult Dogs 73
Meeting New People 76
Cavaliers and Children 77

CHAPTER 8

Cavaliers and Your Other Pets 78
Interspecies Introductions 78
Introducing an Older Dog 80
Aggression/Bad Behavior 81

Rough Play or Aggression? **83**
Raising Multiple Puppies from the Same Litter **84**

CHAPTER 9
Exercising Your Cavalier **86**
Exercise Requirements **86**
How to Make Exercise Fun **87**
Importance of Mental Exercise **88**
Tips for Keeping Your Cavalier Occupied **89**
    Rotate Toys **91**

CHAPTER 10
Training Your Cavalier King Charles Spaniel **92**
Benefits of Proper Training **93**
Training Your Cavalier at Home **94**
Maintaining Clear Expectations **95**
Basic Commands **96**
Training Methods **98**
    Alpha Dog Training **98**
Positive Reinforcement **99**
    Primary Reinforcement **100**
    Secondary Reinforcement **100**
Dangers of Correcting by Punishment **100**
When to Hire a Trainer **101**

CHAPTER 11
Grooming Your Cavalier **102**
Coat Basics **102**
Basic Grooming Tools **103**
Bathing and Brushing **103**
Nail Trimming **105**
Cleaning the Ears and Eyes **106**
Dental Care **107**
To Clip or Not to Clip **108**
When to Seek Professional Help **109**

CHAPTER 12
Basic Health Care **110**
Visiting the Vet **110**
Fleas and Ticks **111**
Vaccinations **114**

Common Diseases and Conditions **115**
   Mitral Valve Disease **115**
   Patellar Luxation **116**
   Syringomyelia **116**
   Epilepsy **116**
   Hip Dysplasia **116**
   Other Notable Diseases **117**
Holistic Alternatives and Supplements **117**
Pet Insurance **119**

CHAPTER 13
Nutrition **120**
Benefits of Quality Dog Food **120**
Types of Commercial Dog Foods **121**
Ingredients to Avoid **122**
   BHA/ BHT **122**
   Meat, Meat Meal, or Rendered Fat **123**
   Nitrites and Nitrates **123**
   Soy **123**
Homemade Dog Food **125**
Table Food **125**
Weight Management **126**

CHAPTER 14
Dealing with Unwanted Behaviors **128**
What Is Considered Bad Behavior? **128**
Finding the Root of the Problem **131**
How to Properly Correct Your Dog **133**
When to Call a Professional **133**

CHAPTER 15
Caring for Your Senior Cavalier **134**
Common Old-Age Ailments **134**
Basic Senior Dog Care **136**
Illness and Injury Prevention **137**
Supplements and Nutrition **137**
When It's Time to Say Goodbye **138**
How will you know when the time is right? **139**
The Euthanasia Process **139**
   Golden Eyes **141**

Special Thanks:

A debt of gratitude is owed to Charlie Weidig of BlackFire Cavaliers for his help and exceptional contributions to this book. Your expertise and advice were a vital resource and I am extremely grateful and honored to have had your help.

CHAPTER 1
Breed History

What Is a Cavalier King Charles Spaniel?

"Cavaliers are such a great family dog, and will give constant companionship to all who walk through the door. They are also great with other dogs and cats. Basically they just get along with anyone or anything."

Kacey Leitheiser
Kacey's Cavaliers

The Cavalier King Charles Spaniel is a breed that commands attention wherever it goes. Its regal appearance attracts onlookers, adult and child alike. It seems no one can resist those big, curious brown eyes. The Cavalier has piqued the interest of royals throughout history for many reasons, but it is impossible to deny that this quintessential lapdog is about as sweet as they come.

Photo Courtesy of Jade Bromley

Photo Courtesy of
Katherine Eastman

History of the Cavalier

"The Cavalier King Charles Spaniel acquired its name because it was a great favorite of King Charles I of Britain in the 1600s."

Jenn Brisco
Cardinal Cavaliers

The origins of the Cavalier King Charles Spaniel have been traced back to the 16th century, when the first toy spaniels are thought to have been brought to Europe from East Asia. These dogs had domed heads, high-set ears, and pointed noses. It is believed these spaniels shared origins with the Pekingese and Japanese Chin. Commonly used by upper-class women as lap warmers and flea catchers, these dogs quickly gained favor with the royals of Europe.

The toy spaniel first appeared in England in 1558 in a painting of Queen Mary I and King Phillip. This new spaniel-type dog was also a favorite of Mary, Queen of Scots, and King Frances III of France. It wasn't until the 17th century that the breed began to rise in popularity because of King Charles

Photo Courtesy of
Victoria Harbottle

II. He was well known for his love of the breed and is said to have allowed the dogs to roam freely at Whitehall Palace, even during palace events.

Samuel Pepys, a member of Parliament during the reign of Charles II, wrote, "All I observed there was the silliness of the King, playing with his dog all the while and not minding the business."

The toy spaniel continued to grow in popularity in Europe and

FUN FACT
Companion of Royals

Often in the company of royalty in historic paintings, the Cavalier was favored by Mary, Queen of Scots, and King Charles I. It is said that Mary's spaniel hid beneath her skirts as she was executed, faithful to the end. The breed's name is derived from King Charles I and his son Charles II of England.

was frequently featured in art and literature. It wasn't until after the Glorious Revolution in 1668 that the breed began to see dramatic changes in its physical characteristics. Around this time, the Pug was introduced to Britain. As the Pug gained popularity among the upper class, the toy spaniel was bred to the Pug in order to create the flatter nose and rounded head that was trendy at the time. The spaniel now featured a rounded head, short, flattened snout, and large round eyes; these dogs no longer resembled King Charles II's dogs.

In 1903, Edward VII named the breed the King Charles Spaniel, based on that monarch's renowned love of the dogs. Over twenty years later in 1926, an American, Eldridge Roswell, wanted to revive the old look of the breed as seen in paintings from Charles II's era. He challenged breeders and offered a prize for the best "Blenheim Spaniels of the old type, as shown in pictures of Charles II of England's time, long face, no stop, flat skull, not inclined to be domed, with spot in centre of skull." Eldridge died before seeing the Cavalier come to life, but interest in this "old type" spaniel had regained attention.

The prize money was awarded to a dog named Ann's Son in 1928. That same year, the first Cavalier club was created. Ann's Son was a living specimen at the Cavalier Club meeting where the breed standard was set for the breed recognized by the Kennel Club as King Charles Spaniel, Cavalier type.

In 1952, the first Cavalier was brought to America. It was a black and tan bitch given to Mrs. Sally Lyons Brown. Cavalier King Charles Spaniel Club USA was founded in 1954, and incorporated in 1956. The breed went on to gain recognition from the American Kennel Club in 1995 and has gained popularity in the United States ever since.

Photo Courtesy of
Joanna Loomes

Physical Characteristics

*"Most people don't realize that the Cavalier type of Spaniel, so pop-
ular in England in the 16th to 18th Century (and seen in classical paintings of that period) actually disappeared in the 19th Century, when their
characteristics were bred out, and the English Toy Spaniel emerged. It
was only in the early half of the 20th Century that the breed was recreat-
ed through careful breeding, and today's Cavalier was not generally seen
in the United States until the second half of the 1900s."*

Charles Weidig
BlackFire Cavaliers

The Cavalier King Charles Spaniel is one of the largest Toy breeds in the
group as determined by the American Kennel Club. Breed standard says the
Cavalier should stand between 12 and 13 inches tall and weigh between 13
and 18 pounds. The head should be proportionate to the dog, not appear-
ing too large or too small. Head should be rounded but not domed, almost
flat on the top and ears set high but not too close. Ears should be long and
have lots of feathering, a key identifier for the breed

A Cavalier's eyes are one of its most prominent features. The eyes
should be round and large but not protruding. They are a deep, dark brown
with a dark rim. Cushioning below the eyes is what contributes to the gentle, melting expression they are known for.

The muzzle is full but tapered slightly and should measure about 1.5
inches from the stop to the tip of the nose. The tail should be carried happily but not much above the level of the back. The coat is of moderate length,
slightly wavy but with no curl. For competition purposes, the silky coat must
never be trimmed except for between the pads of the feet. Long feathering
should be present on the ears, tail, chest, legs, and feet.

The Cavalier appears in four distinct color patterns: Blenheim, Tricolor,
Ruby, and Black and Tan.

Blenheim – Named after Blenheim Palace, Blenheim is the most popular Cavalier. This coat features a rich chestnut color broken up on a pearly
white background. Ears are covered in chestnut and both eyes are surrounded, evenly spaced with white blaze between the eyes and ears. Some
Blenheims feature the desirable lozenge or "Blenheim spot" between the
ears on the center of the head.

Black and Tan – Black and tan presents as jet black with tan markings over the eyes, cheeks, chest, legs, inside ears, and on the underside of the tail.

Tricolor – Tricolor presents as jet black markings broken up on a pearly white background with rich tan markings over the eyes, on the cheeks, inside the ears, and on the underside of the tail. The ears are black and both eyes surrounded with a white blaze between them.

Ruby – Solid colored red. No markings or spots.

Typical Breed Behavior

"The Cavalier King Charles Spaniel is an active, graceful, well-balanced toy spaniel, very gay and free in action; fearless and sporting in character, yet at the same time gentle and affectionate. It is this typical gay temperament, combined with true elegance and royal appearance which are of paramount importance in the breed. Natural appearance with no trimming, sculpting or artificial alteration is essential to breed type."

AKC breed standard

The Cavalier King Charles Spaniel was bred for companionship and warmth, two words that still accurately describe this breed today. Cavaliers don't require much in the way of physical exercise but they make up for it in time needed with their owners. Prized for their lovable temperament, the American Kennel Club describes them as "gay, friendly, non-aggressive with no tendency towards nervousness or shyness."

The Cavalier is a highly adaptable breed that can thrive in almost any situation. Descended from the sporty spaniel, the Cavalier can be athletic and energetic and has been known to compete successfully in agility shows. On the other hand, Cavaliers are

HELPFUL TIP
A People Dog

The Cavalier King Charles Spaniel enjoys the company of humans. Just waiting for a lap to sit in, your Cavalier will follow you throughout your day until you pause and invite him to sit on your knee. Since the breed typically does not like to be alone for long periods of time, the ideal owner would be a stay-at-home parent, someone who works from home, or a retired person or couple.

perfectly content snoozing on the couch or in their owners' laps all day.

Photo Courtesy of Jacqui Wicks

Cavaliers' friendly nature makes them great dogs to keep in a household with mixed breeds. They get along fantastically with all dogs, both big and small, but do possess an undeniable instinct to chase things including small animals, birds, and even cars, so you may want to keep Mr. Hamster separated.

Cavaliers' highly adaptable and non-aggressive nature makes them the perfect family dog for anyone. They love all people, from small children to the elderly, and make a great companion pet for the disabled who may not be able to supply sufficient exercise to a more demanding breed of dog.

Loving and loyal, the Cavalier loves to show affection to all, including the burglar trying to break into your house while you are gone. There are so many things the Cavalier is praised for, but the breed's ability to guard and protect a home is not one of them. For many people, it's a trade-off they are willing to take for the unconditional companionship of this adoring breed.

"Cavaliers are called 'the comforter spaniels'. They are very childlike and really enjoy the company of their family. They have the sweetest dispositions and can adapt to most environments. They are devoted to family members and love children and adults of any age. They require a lot of love and give it in return."

Margaret Hubbard
Lanmar Cavaliers

Is the Cavalier the Right Breed for You?

"Cavaliers are a well rounded breed. They can go for long walk with you or just sit on the couch. They enjoy agility, conformation, nose work, being a therapy dog or even hunting. Cavaliers just love to please you and be with you."

Linda Jones
Lyncrest Cavaliers

If you're looking for a beautiful dog that offers love, affection, and endless cuddle time, the Cavalier King Charles Spaniel is the right breed for you! Easy to please and equally eager to please, the Cavalier can live anywhere. This includes apartments, houses with yards, or even recreational vehicles for the most adventurous travel types.

If you plan to let your Cavalier roam freely in the yard, make certain that his area is securely fenced with no openings. Cavaliers love to meet people, and they will escape from the yard if given the opportunity. Once free, a Cavalier will seek out new friends, and will happily go off with anyone who appears to be a good human companion.

If you live in an apartment, or do not have a securely fenced yard, plan on walking your Cavalier on a lead several times a day. Fortunately, it's an activity that they love.

Cavaliers offer friendship to young children and can be a fun way to teach them valuable life lessons and responsibilities. The forgiving nature of these dogs helps them play the role of family pet flawlessly and with grace, but it is worth considering that small children can sometimes injure smaller dogs and puppies unintentionally with extra tight hugs or too-firm pats. Always be sure to teach your children to be gentle so they don't accidentally injure your Cavalier.

Requiring little physical exercise, Cavaliers require more than average time with their owners. Companionship is of utmost importance for the breed and your dog will suffer if left alone too often.

Cavaliers enjoy engaging in fun activities with their owners. Your puppy will learn from a very early age that he can fetch a ball or toy thrown by his human companion, and bring it back for another go at it. The little bit of exercise from these short bursts of energy will help keep him fit and healthy into old age.

Before bringing your Cavalier home, it's important to carefully consider all aspects of Cavalier ownership. Taking on a dog of any breed, even the most easygoing, presents challenges and frustrations. Can you afford to care for your dog? Do you have the time to devote to it? Are there any restrictions where you live? If you are willing to understand and prepare for the dog you choose, the transition into puppy parenthood should be a smooth one.

Cost of Ownership

Because of the relative rarity of this breed, the average price of a Cavalier puppy from a reputable breeder is going to be anywhere from $2,500 to $6,000, depending on the breeder you choose. The price of each puppy will depend on a few factors including color, sex, and lineage. Typically, a female or male Blenheim is going to demand the highest price tag.

Purchase price is not the only cost to consider. The first year of a dog's life can be expensive. When you consider the supplies you will need to buy, veterinary visits and training classes, the cost can really add up. Most puppies come with their first round of shots but you will need to be sure they get the rest from a vet. It is also important to remember, unless you plan to breed your Cavalier, that the cost of a spay or neuter can vary depending on location but generally costs $75 to $250 or more.

Because the Cavalier is a smaller breed, the dogs cost on average $200 to $400 to feed a year, depending on the food. The premium dog food brands may seem expensive, but they will ultimately lead to better health and overall quality of life.

Cavaliers' regal coats are a thing of beauty, but they are not without maintenance. Cavaliers are prone to mats and need to be brushed often to keep their coats clean and looking their best. According to the American Kennel Club, the Cavalier should never be clipped but if you don't think you will be able to keep up with the regular bath and brush, consider hiring a professional groomer to keep your dog in tip-top shape.

The Cavalier King Charles Spaniel is not a dog suitable for everyone. The cost of the dog alone can be significantly higher than other breeds. However, if you are financially able to purchase and care for a Cavalier, he will reward you with ultimate loyalty, love, and companionship for the rest of his life.

CHAPTER 2
Choosing Your Cavalier

"A Cavalier who follows the Breed Standard should be fearless in character, while at the same time gentle and affectionate. Cavaliers bond strongly with their human partners, and enjoy nothing more than doing things with them, or just sitting on their human's lap. They are sporting in nature, and enjoy playing games, doing tricks, or taking part in any other activity that pleases their human partner."

Charles Weidig
BlackFire Cavaliers

Buying vs. Adopting

Deciding whether to purchase your Cavalier from a breeder or adopt from a rescue can be a tough decision. We all have our heartstrings plucked when we see commercials showing dogs in need but oftentimes these dogs have special needs, medical or social, and require a special kind of home. If you think you can provide the patience and care it may take to adopt a rescue Cavalier, please do so! The dog will reward you with love and companionship just as much as one you raise from a puppy.

One key benefit to adopting an older Cavalier is having the chance to learn the dog's personality before you bring him home. You'll know ahead of time if the dog enjoys the company of young children or other dogs, what level of exercise this particular dog expects, and exactly how to handle any medical or social issues he may have. There are very few surprises when it comes to adopting a well-established, older Cavalier.

A rescue dog often seems to show a special appreciation for a new chance at a forever home. If you're looking to adopt a Cavalier and happen to find one at a rescue that has no special needs, chances are the dog will be adopted fast, so don't hesitate to get your application in!

Importance of Breeder Reputation

"Finding the right breeder is important because you may have questions all through your Cavaliers life and you will want a breeder that will be there to help you answer those questions."

Linda Jones
Lyncrest Cavaliers

Finding a trustworthy breeder can be a challenge when there are so many questionable breeders out there. People will pay good money for a purebred dog and this has caused many to take up "backyard breeding." Oftentimes these breeders do little or no testing to ensure the health of their litters. Some of these places even turn out to be puppy mills. These are places where dogs are kept alive to do nothing more than pump out litter after litter. Often kept in small cages in unclean conditions, this is a terrible life for a dog! Avoiding supporting places like this is just as important as ensuring the health of your puppy.

A good, reputable breeder will be known as such in the Cavalier breeder community. They will undoubtedly have connections with other reputable breeders. If you find a good breeder who has no current available puppies, you may want to contact them and ask for the names of other breeders in the area. A reputable breeder is always concerned with breeding dogs up to the standard of the breed and should only recommend the same.

Photo Courtesy of
Dina Baričić

Finding the Right Breeder

"Choosing the right breeder is an important part of getting a puppy. You want to find a breeder that does health clearances on both parents and takes the puppies for vet checks and shots before sending the puppies home with their new families. You should be able to go see the puppies and parents of the puppies before purchasing. Searching the internet for Cavalier puppies at low prices is not the way to start. Find reputable breeders through the Cavalier King Charles Spaniel Club. www.ckcsc.org"

Margaret Hubbard
Lanmar Cavaliers

The internet makes finding a reputable breeder easier than ever and yet challenging at the same time. If you do a quick internet search for "Cavalier puppies for sale," you will find a whole slew of breeders. Some of these, no doubt, you will want to avoid. So how can you tell the difference between a reputable breeder and someone who is just trying to make a quick buck without any care for the well-being of the breed?

There are a number of questions you should ask any breeder when you are searching for the perfect Cavalier puppy.

Photo Courtesy of
Susanna Collier

Photo Courtesy of Sunna Gautadóttir

Can I visit the breeding facility?

The answer to this question should always be yes. For safety issues regarding the new puppies, a breeder may not allow you into certain areas of the facility. There is a concern of tracking in diseases that could be detrimental to a young puppy's undeveloped immune system. However, a quality breeder should always allow you to come on site and see other dogs in their program. If they refuse, this could be a sign they have something to hide and you should reconsider.

How long have you been breeding Cavaliers?

You will want to buy from an experienced breeder who is well established so the answer to this question should be several years. A quality breeder who has several years of experience will know all the ins and outs of breeding for only the most desirable traits and healthy dogs.

What genetic conditions do you test for before breeding and what conditions do you screen the puppies for before selling?

There are numerous genetic conditions that Cavaliers are prone to developing. The most problematic among the breed are defects of the heart that can be fatal. Before agreeing to purchase a puppy, ask for a

PETNAP 36" x 36" WHELPING BOX
www.petnap.co.uk

Photo Courtesy of
Gayle Seale

detailed list of the tests the breeder performed on the parents and ask for copies of the test results. These tests should be performed by certified specialists for each potential ailment such as a board-certified veterinarian cardiologist for the heart and a board-certified ophthalmologist for conditions of the eyes. Just because the breeder had the dogs checked out by a general veterinarian does not mean they were genetically tested to know if they are likely to pass undesirable traits down to their offspring.

Can I see veterinary records for both parents?

When investing thousands of dollars into a Cavalier puppy, you will want to have an open and transparent line of communication with your chosen breeder. If the breeder is not willing to share medical records of the puppy's parents, this may be a signal you should find another breeder. Both the dam and the sire should have been checked by specialists and cleared for defects as well as have proof of genetic testing.

What kind of guarantee do you provide for your puppies?

A good breeder will always guarantee the health of their puppies. Look for guarantees that will refund most or all of the cost of the puppy in the event any congenital health conditions appear within the first year. Beware of breeders who only offer to replace the puppy with a healthy one with no option to receive a refund instead. If the breeder produced a genetically unhealthy puppy the first time, why would you want to bring home another puppy from the same place? Many people are also unwilling to return their dog for a replacement as they have already become attached. This is a low-risk guarantee from a breeder and may be a warning sign. On the other hand, a responsible breeder will always take back a dog that you can no longer care for, no matter the reason.

Oftentimes a breeder's health guarantee will have stipulations. These may include not neutering or spaying until after a year so the joints are allowed to fully develop, feeding your puppy a proper diet, and regular visits to the vet. As much as a responsible breeder wants their puppies to remain in perfect health for their entire life, not all owners care for a dog the same way and health results will vary based on lifestyle.

Remember, no matter how good the breeding lines are or how thorough the testing, a puppy is a living creature and diseases can develop. No breeder can guarantee perfect health for a dog's entire life. If something does go wrong with your puppy, before putting the blame on the breeder, it is important to understand any role you may have unwittingly played in the situation.

Do you ever sell to a broker or pet shop?

If the answer is yes, walk away from this breeder immediately and do not support them. A responsible breeder, breeding for the betterment of the Cavalier's health and appearance, would never sell one of their animals to a broker or a pet store. Reputable breeders want to meet the families of each of their puppies to be sure they will

HELPFUL TIP
Breeders

The hunt for reputable breeders of the Cavalier King Charles Spaniel should begin with a search on the website of the American Kennel Club (akc.org). Here you can search by champion bloodlines and find a reputable breeder in your geographical area. The "Parent Club," the American Cavalier King Charles Spaniel Club, Inc., can be found at ackcsc.org.

Photo Courtesy of Sara Gregor

be properly cared for. Puppies found in a pet shop are bred for profit alone and will come with no health guarantee and many potential problems.

Respected Breeder Charles Weidig of BlackFire Cavaliers offers his top three tips for choosing the right breeder:

1. Make certain the breeder you choose follows a thorough health testing protocol on the parents of your puppy. In the process of producing any purebred animal, it is necessary to do a certain amount of inbreeding. Although this is necessary to produce the desirable traits of the breed, it also tends to increase the incidence of certain health problems. Fortunately, if a disease is genetic, the probability that it will occur can be minimized by testing and clearing the parents that are used for breeding. In Cavaliers, there are four major inherited health concerns: heart disease (specifically Mitral Valve Disease), eye problems, hip dysplasia, and patella luxation. Responsible breeders wait until their Cavaliers are old enough (over 2 years old) for these problems to be diagnosed if they are present, and if not present, they will obtain clearances from specialists. The Orthopedic Foundation For Animals (www.ofa. org) maintains a registry where breeders may file their dogs' health test results, and where you can easily search to see the latest health clearances on the parents of any puppy you are interested in. For breeders who do not use OFA, ask to see copies of the latest health test results.

2. Try to locate a breeder who is actively engaged in exhibiting his/her Cavaliers at dog shows, preferably in both the AKC and the Cavalier King Charles Spaniel Club USA. Breeders who show their dogs are far more concerned that any puppies they produce have the true look, structure, and temperament of a Cavalier than those who breed simply to sell puppies.

3. Visit the breeder's home before making a commitment. You should be able to meet the mother of the litter, and meet all Cavaliers in the breeder's possession. Make certain that they live in the home as part of the family, not kept in a kennel outdoors or in the basement.

Picking the Perfect Puppy

"Puppies and dogs have different personalities. It's important to share your household personalities and routine with the breeder or group to find the right match."

Christine Vitolo
Royal Flush Cavaliers

Although temperament and behavior characteristics should be relatively consistent throughout a well-bred litter of Cavaliers, individual puppy personalities will vary. If possible, visit your breeder's facility before take-home day to pick out your new puppy. Often, breeders have waiting lists of people hoping to purchase a puppy from their next litter. It's important, once you have chosen a reputable breeder, to get on the list as soon as possible. This will allow you the best possible chance of getting an early pick from the litter.

If you are able to visit the litter beforehand, there are a few things to keep in mind. If the puppies are all playing together, does one seem more aggressive than another? This one may be feisty, energetic, and a bit more assertive by nature. Is there one who would rather play alone in the corner with her own toy? This puppy may be a bit more docile and independent. Is there one that is climbing all over you, gnawing on your hands or shoes? This could be a puppy with a naturally more curious and adventurous personality. None of these personalities are better or worse than the other, but you should have a type of dog in mind that you are hoping for so that you can make the best choice for your family and for your future puppy.

If you are unsure which puppy you should choose, ask the breeder for help. They are the ones who have spent the most time with the puppies and at this point they should have a pretty good idea of each of their personalities.

Tips for Adopting a Cavalier

"If you choose to adopt, be aware that Cavaliers have a number of health issues. Without a lot of history on a rescue or adoptee, be sure you are prepared to embrace financially and emotionally whatever illness or disease may come along with your new friend."

Brooke N.
Painted Blessing's Cavaliers

If you have your heart set on adopting a Cavalier King Charles Spaniel, there are a number of resources available to you. First, check with Cavalier Rescue USA. They have numerous Cavaliers to choose from by region with detailed descriptions about each dog. You can also check with any reputable Cavalier breeder. They should know if there are any local rescues in your area. Remember that the overwhelming majority of rescue Cavaliers will be elderly, disabled, chronically ill, or all of the above. The majority of these dogs have been turned in because their owners can't afford the time or money it takes to care for an ailing, poor-bred dog. While the dogs will present special challenges to care for, they will still provide you with the loyal companionship and love that is so engrained in the Cavalier nature.

CHAPTER 3
Preparing for Your Cavalier

Before bringing home your Cavalier, be sure to prepare your home and your family. Puppy pick-up day is exciting for everyone but there is nothing worse than getting your new puppy home and then realizing you are not quite ready for the new arrival! By taking the time to get everything in order before you bring home your puppy, the first few days with your new Cavalier will go much smoother.

Preparing Children and Other Pets

"Introductions with existing pets should be slow and monitored. Cavaliers are friendly, loving and playful so it's often up to the established pet on when things get settled."

Christine Vitolo
Royal Flush Cavaliers

If you are bringing your new puppy home to a house with no children or other pets, the transition should be a relatively easy one. If you do have children or other pets, you must make careful preparations to allow everyone time to adjust. In regards to children, depending on their age, the only preparations needed will be to teach them gentle handling of your future puppy. Most children are excited and cannot wait to get their new puppy, so adjusting them to the idea should be a breeze. Cavaliers in general are more delicately built dogs, so it is especially important to show children how to safely hold, pick up, and pet your Cavalier puppy. Often, a small child can harm a puppy unintentionally by trying to show affection in a manner too rough. Careful supervision

Photo Courtesy of Suzanne Karpov

should be maintained with small children and puppies, even if you think they understand.

Photo Courtesy of
Jessica Ann Galvin

When it comes to adjusting your current pets to the idea of a new puppy, things may get a little more complicated. Depending on the type of pets and their nature, the transition may be simple or it may take a little extra work.

If you have another dog or multiple, warming them up to the idea of a new puppy before the introduction is a good idea. Discuss this transition with your chosen breeder and see if they will allow you to pick up a blanket or a toy with the new puppy's scent on it. Introduce the blanket or toy to your current dog or dogs and allow them to become accustomed to the smell of another puppy in the house.

When you pick up your new puppy, have someone help you with the first introduction. If possible, let your dogs meet your new puppy in a neutral area where your current pets will be less likely to be territorial. Because your puppy's immune system is not fully developed, you will not want to take your new puppy to a park or another public place, but you may consider letting them meet briefly outside of the house in a less used area. Keep your dogs leashed but give them a bit of slack so they can greet the puppy. Keep a close eye on all parties during the introduction to ensure the safety of your new puppy. Keep the first meeting brief and then separate your dogs from the new puppy so they do not overwhelm each other. After you see how they react to each other, you can slowly allow them to spend more time together until they are completely acclimated and coexisting in harmony.

If you are introducing your puppy to a resident cat, it's important to keep both your cat and puppy safe by maintaining control of your puppy or by allowing them to meet while one animal is contained by a crate or another barrier. Allow them short, controlled interactions at quiet moments of the day until they are both calm around each other.

A new puppy can be exciting and become the focal point of life for a while. Remember to show your other dogs and pets some extra attention and love so they know that they are still important members of the family.

Photo Courtesy of Danielle Scattergood

Puppy-Proofing Your Home

"Puppy proof your house! Remove all small items that are within reach, puppies will want to chew on anything that they can get their mouth on. Also, determine a designated area for the puppy; do not give a puppy full access to the entire house. You cannot watch a puppy at all times. When the puppy is not under your full attention and observation it needs to be in its own confined space."

Mark Fitchpatrick
Briarcliff Cavaliers

One of the first things you should do in preparation for your new Cavalier is to puppy-proof your home. There are many seemingly ordinary things in your home that could prove hazardous to the new addition to the family.

Hide or remove any electrical cords within the puppy's reach. Puppies are curious little creatures who love to explore, oftentimes with their mouths. If you cannot remove the cords from your puppy's reach, you may want to invest in some cord protectors. These cord wraps usually come infused with bitter flavors to help deter chewing. If you find you have a particularly stubborn chewer, you can spritz the cords with no-chew spray, found in pet stores, to ensure he will not find the cord appealing anymore.

Invest in fully enclosed trash cans if you do not have them already. Keeping the kitchen trash out of reach may be a no brainer but even the smaller trash cans around your bathrooms and office are tempting playthings for a small, curious Cavalier. Sometimes a used cotton swab or a wad of paper is just too irresistible not to chew up.

Put up all medications, chemicals, and cleaning supplies. If you tend to keep any medications in an area that your puppy may be able to reach, be sure to move those to a higher location such as a dedicated medicine cabinet. As mentioned above, puppies explore everything with their mouths and

HELPFUL TIP
Off to a Good Start

Before you bring your new Cavalier home, give a great deal of thought to where you will house your pet. You will want to have a dedicated area in your home near the exit you will use to take your dog outside to relieve itself. This space should contain enough room for your pet's bed, water dish, favorite toys, and litter pan spot.

Photo Courtesy of
Jette Løfstedt

snatching a bottle or box of medication off the sofa table could prove to be fatal for your new puppy. Also, move any chemicals, cleaning supplies, dish pods, or laundry detergents into an enclosed area and out of reach. This includes any rat bait or poisons that your new puppy may find enticing. Even if you think these items are in an area of the house your puppy will not be allowed, it only takes one escape for your new Cavalier to encounter something detrimental.

Watch out for poisonous house plants. House plants may seem innocent but not all are the same. Some houseplants are actually poisonous and can cause serious issues for a nibbling puppy. Some of the most common houseplants that are potentially dangerous for your new puppy are the Corn Plant, Sago Palm, Aloe, and Jade Plant. To find a complete list, visit the ASPCA website.

Beware of xylitol. Xylitol is considered a sugar alcohol and is commonly found in items throughout almost every household. As people become more and more aware of the dangers of added sugars, companies are turning to xylitol, an additive that tastes sweet but does not spike blood sugar and insulin levels like sugar. Xylitol can be found in almost anything but is most commonly found in chewing gum, mints, candies, toothpaste and even peanut butter. Xylitol is highly toxic to dogs and can cause dangerously low blood sugar levels resulting in weakness, seizures, trembling, or even death. When dogs consume very high levels of xylitol, it may cause necrosis of the liver which often leads to death.

Be sure to keep all purses and bags which may contain gum, candies, or toothpaste up and out of reach of your puppy at all times. Have a designated area for guests' bags so they are not accidentally left within reach. Also, check all food labels for xylitol before giving your puppy a special treat. It is often recommended to give a dog peanut butter to help them take any medication but be sure to check that your peanut butter does not contain xylitol first.

Keep the batteries away. While you probably don't have random batteries lying around on the floor, you may have remotes or small electronic toys. If your puppy is able to get ahold of a battery-operated remote or toy, he could potentially chew them enough to expose the battery. Small button cell batteries are the most dangerous as they are small enough for your puppy to swallow. Swallowing a battery is a serious, life-threatening issue and can cause internal burns. Call the nearest emergency vet immediately if you suspect your puppy may have swallowed a battery.

Put away any children's toys. Children's toys are often made up of small pieces that are a choking hazard to your dog. Be especially careful with toys that contain magnets inside as these pose an extra risk of internal damage when more than one is consumed.

Set up puppy gates. After you have puppy-proofed your entire house, you should designate a safe common area for your puppy to stay. Use puppy gates to block any doorways or staircases so it will be easier for you to keep a close eye on your new Cavalier. Having already puppy-proofed the entire house, you can be sure that even if your Cavalier makes a great escape into a room he is not allowed, the dangerous items have all been removed.

It only takes one second for your new Cavalier to get into something that could cause him harm, so it is extremely important you notify everyone in the house of the changes being made before your puppy comes home.

Dangerous Things Your Dog Might Eat

"Puppies are just like babies. Anything on the floor goes in their mouth. Electrical cords should be raised or removed. Any small objects should always be picked up. Check for poisonous house plants and remove them."

Margaret Hubbard
Lanmar Cavaliers

Although feeding your dog food from the table is not recommended, it's often difficult to resist those begging eyes looking up at you while you eat. If you do get the urge to toss your pup a little treat, make sure you know what he can and can't have. There are a number of foods, perfectly healthy for humans, that can and do cause illness or toxicity in dogs.

Chocolate – A crowd favorite among humans, chocolate can cause major issues for your loving Cavalier. Chocolate contains methylxanthines, which are a stimulant that can stop a dog's metabolic process. Methylxanthines are found in especially high amounts in pure dark chocolate and baker's chocolate. Consuming too much methylxanthine causes seizures and irregular heart function which can lead to death.

Xylitol – As discussed above, xylitol is particularly dangerous to dogs as it does not take much to cause a dangerous or deadly reaction. Vomiting is typically the initial symptom of xylitol poisoning. If you suspect there is a chance your dog has ingested even a small amount of xylitol, call the veterinarian immediately because time is critical.

Raw or Cooked Bones – Raw or cooked bones are a choking hazard for your dog. The bones can break or splinter and become lodged or worse, puncture their digestive tract. This is especially true with cooked bones of any kind as they become dry and brittle. Pork and poultry bones are especially dangerous as they are more likely to splinter and cause issues.

Though controversial, some veterinarians say that raw bones of the right variety can provide healthy nutrients and help prevent tartar and plaque build-up in the mouth. These bones are recommended only under very close supervision and only for a few minutes at a time, placing the bone in the refrigerator for a maximum of four days before discarding. If the bone is breaking or if your dog seems to be swallowing any pieces, discard the bone immediately. If you prefer to skip the risk, look for bones in the pet store that are meant to withstand heavy chewing without breaking.

Other foods that may cause gastrointestinal upset or worse for your dog are grapes and raisins, certain nuts including macadamia nuts, avocados, apple cores and seeds, and anything in the allium family including onions and garlic. This is not a comprehensive list so it is best to check with your veterinarian before giving anything from your plate to your dog.

Supplies to Purchase Before You Bring Your Cavalier Home

Getting ready for a new puppy can be overwhelming. There is so much information to learn and preparations to be made around the house. Gathering all the supplies you need before you bring your puppy home will make the first few days much easier. Follow this list of essentials and you will have all you need for the day you bring your Cavalier home.

Food and water bowl – Food and water bowls come in many shapes, colors, and sizes. They can be made from ceramic, stainless steel, or plastic. When choosing a bowl set for your new puppy, there are a few things to consider. Plastic bowls may come in fun colors and patterns but they are lightweight, easy to tip over, and many puppies think they are fun to chew on. They are also more difficult to clean thoroughly when they become scratched or damaged.

Photo Courtesy of
Kelsey Norris

Ceramic bowls are heavier, less likely to be tipped over, and are easier to clean than plastic. They are breakable, though, so if your puppy does manage to knock it over and move it around, it is likely to chip or break.

Stainless-steel bowls are both easy to clean and unbreakable so even if they are tipped over and kicked around, they shouldn't get damaged. You can also buy these bowls with wide rubber or silicone bases to stop sliding and prevent tipping.

A bowl with a diameter of no more than 5 inches is ideal for a Cavalier; this is the perfect size for an adult, allowing the long ears to fall outside the bowl while he is eating. If food gets on his ears, he may spend time chewing at it, gnawing off the beautiful long feathering that is characteristic of the breed.

Another option you will find in a pet store is an elevated bowl set. These are bowls that are set up off the floor so that your dog doesn't have to bend over as far to eat. Created to try to help prevent the serious issue of bloat in some breeds, studies have actually shown that elevated feeders can potentially contribute to bloat. Since this is not usually a common issue for smaller dog breeds such as the Cavalier, an elevated feeder is unnecessary and some would say potentially problematic. If you are adopting an older Cavalier that has neck or mobility issues, then an elevated dog feeder would be something to discuss with your veterinarian as an option.

Collar, tags, and leash – One of the first things you will want to do when you get your new puppy is put on his or her collar with identification tags. These tags can be made at any local pet store or you can order one from an online retailer. It's best to always have your pet's name, your current address, and phone number on the tag. This is meant to help a stranger return your dog in the event he ever gets lost. You can even add a little note that says "Please Call My Family."

Food – Your breeder should send a small amount of food home with your puppy to get you through the first couple of days. It would be best to continue with this same brand of food as it is probably a high-quality brand and will save your puppy any intestinal upset from switching. If you do want to switch foods, talk with your breeder about how to do it safely. They will probably recommend you switch gradually by mixing in the puppy's current food with the new food over a period of a several days.

Puppy-safe toys – Your puppy will have lots of energy and very sharp teeth. In order to save your couch legs and your shoes, you will want to have at least four or five different dog toys for your puppy to choose from. Because you do not yet know what your puppy will prefer, get at least one

Photo Courtesy of
Gail Walker

plush toy, one rubber toy or bone, one rope, and one ball. Buy toys with different squeaker sounds and textures to see which one your puppy will love the most. You may find that plush toys don't last long before being ripped to shreds or you may find that your new puppy loves carrying that stuffed elephant all around the house!

Grooming brush – Cavaliers have high grooming demands and need to be brushed frequently to prevent matting. As a puppy, your Cavalier will not need the brushing his future coat will demand, but it's a good idea to get him used to the brush right from the start to avoid any anxiety or issues with it later. Start with a small, basic medium-bristle brush. A slicker brush, which has wire bristles, can be useful for keeping the ears and other feathering mat-free. Be sure to introduce your puppy to it gently and gradually, so he does not develop a fear of being groomed. Likewise, a sturdy metal comb can also help keep his coat smooth and silky.

Puppy training treats – To help with potty-training and teaching basic commands, it is essential to have a bag of treats. Look for soft treats that are healthy and natural. Be sure that they contain no animal by-product, are grain-free, and have no artificial flavors, colors, or preservatives.

Crate and pad – Your puppy will need somewhere safe to stay while you are gone or when you can't keep a close eye on him, such as at night. Invest in a quality crate and pad that will be big enough for your fully grown Cavalier and establish it as a safe place early on in the training process. It's ideal to buy a crate pad that is washable and has minimal stuffing because chances are, it will be chewed on at some point.

A crate that measures 13 inches by 22 inches is of sufficient size, even for an adult Cavalier. For a young puppy of 10 or 12 weeks, you may want to use a divider to cut down your puppy's space to an area that's just big enough for him to turn around and lie down. If a puppy has too much space, he may urinate or defecate inside the crate, setting back his housebreaking significantly.

Puppy gate or play pen – You will not want your new puppy to have full range of the house right off the bat. Unless your space allows you to keep your puppy contained in a centralized location, you will probably want to purchase a puppy gate or play pen. The idea is to give your young Cavalier his own designated "safe space" where he can play without constant supervision. A gate that blocks a doorway is a good way to keep your puppy from venturing down a hall, up the stairs, or into a room that is off limits, but it still allows him access to furniture or other things in an area which could potentially become chew-things. A play pen allows much more flexibility as you can move it around wherever inside or outside of the house you will be. A play pen also keeps any furniture from becoming damaged by those razor-sharp puppy teeth.

Preparing an Outdoor Space

Cavaliers are an incredibly adaptable breed that can thrive in almost any setting as long as they have their companion by their side. While they don't need a large yard, it is important to keep any outdoor area you have a dog-friendly zone. Letting your Cavalier exert some energy in the backyard is a great way to keep him healthy and fit, but be sure to take all necessary precautions beforehand to keep your dog safe.

Start preparing your outdoor space ahead of time by removing all chemical products from the area. Any weed or pest killer, fertilizers or other similar products should be placed somewhere the dog cannot reach. If you plan to allow your Cavalier to frolic unsupervised for any period of time, you will need to be sure the yard is secure. Check all fencing to be sure there are no gaps between the fence and the ground. Make sure all gates latch completely and there is no way for your Cavalier to climb or jump over the fence. Always be sure your Cavalier is wearing his collar and tags before allowing him outside for any amount of time.

Just like with indoor plants, some outdoor plants and flowers can prove to be poisonous to your dog. Check the list again against any plants you may have in your garden and replace those that may be harmful with a safe alternative.

CHAPTER 4
Bringing Home Your Cavalier

"Try and bring them home on a long weekend so you can establish a routine and bond as soon as possible."

Brooke N.
Painted Blessing's Cavaliers

There is nothing more exciting than the day you get to pick up your new Cavalier from the breeder! You've done your research, prepared your home and yard, purchased all the needed supplies, and now all that's left is to bring your puppy home. You may find yourself a bit anxious, wondering how everything will go, but if you follow the tips below, pick-up day should be fun, exciting and trouble free.

Photo Courtesy of Claire Findlay

Picking Up Your Cavalier

When you arrive at the breeding facility at your appointed time, your breeder should have the puppy ready to go in a designated pick-up area. He or she may be in a pen playing with other puppies that are leaving on the same day. Try not to let the adorable sight of your new Cavalier keep you from hearing the important information your breeder will give you!

HELPFUL TIP
"Let Sleeping Dogs Lie"

According to the American Pet Products Association, nearly half of all American dog owners allow their dogs to sleep in their beds. Be cautious of this habit if you have asthma or allergies. Known to be snorers, Cavaliers may interfere with your sleep patterns. Once you allow your dog to sleep in your bed, it may be difficult to break the habit.

Before you leave, your breeder should give you detailed information on your puppy's vet records, current shots, future shots, and dewormings. They should remind you of any stipulations of the health guarantee and advise you on a feeding schedule. All of this information as well as breed-specific care tips should be neatly presented in a packet of some sort along with registration papers.

Sometimes a breeder will allow you to take a small blanket or toy home with your dog so that the smell of his litter can comfort him during the transition. If may be beneficial to ask ahead of time if this is an option in order to know if you need to provide the blanket before pick-up day.

The Ride Home

Depending on how far you have to travel to pick up your puppy, you will want to plan accordingly. It's not uncommon for a puppy to get motion sick and vomit on the ride home so you may consider requesting that the breeder withhold food for that morning. Regardless of how long the trip is, you will want to be sure to take a bowl and a bottle of water for your puppy in the case of an unexpected delay like a flat tire.

There are a couple of options when it comes to transporting your new Cavalier. Some people let the puppy ride home in a crate. If you plan to transport the puppy in the crate, place only towels in the bottom of the crate so the crate pad is not soiled on the trip. Also, take care to drive extra smoothly so you do not jostle your puppy any more than necessary.

Photo Courtesy of Claire Nicholls

Some people choose to leave the crate home and transport their new puppy in their arms. This is probably the most comfortable way for your new puppy to travel but do take precautions and cover your lap with towels in case there is any vomiting. Riding home with your puppy in your arms should only be done by a passenger and never the driver. This method is not without risk. A puppy can be killed by the airbag, so you should sit in the backseat for the trip.

Unfortunately, there is currently no proven safe way to transport a dog in a vehicle so one method is not safer than the other. Not all crates will withstand the force of a crash and some can even become more dangerous for your dog in the event of a crash. When not properly secured to the vehicle, the crate can become a projectile, injuring your puppy and possibly other passengers in the car. You can visit the Center for Pet Safety (CPS) website for a list of tested and approved travel crates.

If you are thinking of buying a harness for your dog to use in the car, know that they are not all created equally. The Center for Pet Safety performed a Harness Crashworthiness Study in 2013 and results showed that only one of eleven brands tested performed at the level advertised. Some were even deemed "catastrophic failures." Do diligent research on each brand before making your decision.

Before beginning the journey home, allow your puppy to use the restroom on a patch of grass. Praise him if he does and then begin your trip home. The ride home can be a great bonding opportunity for you and your puppy so enjoy those first moments together as a new family.

The First Night

"Have a crate and get the puppy used to being in there as their safe space. Life is a lot simpler if they are comfortable with their 'home'. I have several crates in my home and they are always open and the dogs go in there for their naps."

Kacey Leitheiser
Kacey's Cavaliers

Before bed, take your puppy outside and wait ten to fifteen minutes for him to relieve himself. If he doesn't go, wait ten minutes and then try again. Repeat this process for however long it takes your puppy to go and then put him directly into the crate for bed with his special blanket or toy from the breeder. It may be helpful for nighttime potty runs if you keep the crate by your bed.

The first night home can be daunting and scary for both you and your puppy. That crate can look awfully lonely and uncomfortable for your new Cavalier. There will probably be a lot of whining and crying for the first few nights. After all, this will be the very first time your puppy has spent the night away from mom and siblings. Although it will be tempting to pull your puppy out of the crate and let him sleep with you, it would be best for everyone if you resist the urge and allow your puppy to self-soothe in the crate.

Remember that your puppy will probably need to be taken outside to relieve himself at least once during the night. If your puppy wakes you in the night, it's best to take him outside and then immediately return him right back

Photo Courtesy of Janie Haigh

Photo Courtesy of
Joyce Kearns

to the crate to sleep. This will teach him that nighttime is for sleeping and not for playing.

If your puppy is having a difficult time sleeping in the crate or is keeping you awake with his crying, try talking to your puppy or rubbing his head through the crate to help calm him. The most important thing you can do in the first few days is to make your puppy feel loved and secure. Bonds you form with each other in the early days will last throughout your dog's lifetime and will make all aspects of dog ownership that much more enjoyable.

After a few nights, the bedtime whining should stop and your puppy should come to find his crate a cozy place to sleep. As you and your puppy both adjust to life with each other, routines will form and things will get much easier.

Choosing the Right Veterinarian

When searching for the perfect veterinarian for your new Cavalier, you may be tempted to go online and read reviews. Beware that not all reviews are an accurate depiction of an establishment. Animals are beloved by their owners and sometimes unfavorable things happen that are out of the veterinarian's control. It is very easy for a heartbroken owner to take to the internet and blame the vet for their unfortunate circumstances when the vet may have had nothing to do with the outcome. Instead, start with word of mouth. Ask fellow dog owners which vet they prefer and which ones they would avoid. Make a list of the most favorable and start with those.

Next, eliminate some off of your list based on location. In an emergency, you will want to have chosen a vet that is nearby. If there are any clinics on your list that you feel are too far in the event of a crisis, cross them off.

Call all the remaining clinics on your list and inquire about their prices. You can get a good comparison by asking what they charge for a round of shots, a spay or neuter, and an x-ray. Make notes of what each clinic charges and how they accept payment. Do they demand it all upfront or do they offer payment plans? Also make note of the friendliness of the office staff when you call. Did they offer the information willingly or seem put out? You don't want to commit to a vet clinic with unhelpful office staff. That could make any visit an unpleasant experience.

You should also ask about the prospective vet's policy in regard to vaccinations. Over-vaccinating can compromise your Cavalier's immune system, but you still want to provide proper protection from infectious diseases. The American Animal Hospital Association's current guidelines recommend that core vaccines (distemper/parvo/parainfluenza/adenovirus and rabies), after the initial puppy shots and 1-year booster, be given **no more often than every 3 years**. Make certain that the vet you choose is aware of these guidelines, and does not insist on vaccinating every year throughout the dog's life. Noncore vaccines (Bordetella, leptospirosis, Lyme) should only be given when warranted; a good vet will help you determine whether or not these vaccines are appropriate for your Cavalier's lifestyle and circumstances.

If after all of the above steps you still haven't decided, call each clinic and ask to make an appointment to visit in person. While on your visits, ask the staff or the vet if they have any other Cavalier King Charles Spaniels as patients or have experience with the breed. You will likely find that one of the offices is a better fit for you and your puppy than the others and your decision will then be easy. It is important to trust your veterinarian and feel comfortable in their clinic so don't settle on a vet without taking all the necessary steps.

The First Vet Visit

Some breeders stipulate that you must take your puppy to the vet within a few days for a check-up. If this is the case, you'll want to call and make an appointment with your chosen vet before you pick up your puppy. Be

Photo Courtesy of Emma Beaton

sure to take all records given to you by the breeder for the vet to include in your Cavalier's file.

The first appointment will typically be a general look-over to make sure your puppy is in good health. Your puppy will be weighed and the vet will examine eyes, ears, nose, heart, and lungs. They will look at your dog's skin and coat condition and examine the teeth and mouth. They may take a stool sample to check for parasites. If it's time for your puppy's next round of shots, they will get them at this appointment.

If vaccines are to be given, make sure that your puppy does not receive more than one vaccine

Photo Courtesy of
Janet Stokesley

in a single visit. In order to preserve the integrity of your puppy's immune system, if a second vaccine is required, it should be given on the next visit. This is a practice that should be followed throughout your Cavalier's life.

The first vet appointment should be relatively quick and easy. Take this opportunity to ask your vet any questions you may have about feeding or caring for your new puppy. If you have made a list of questions, don't be afraid to pull it out and make sure you get thorough answers.

The first few days at home with your new Cavalier puppy will probably be a combination of wonderful and frustrating. You may get a little less sleep than normal, but the bond you and your puppy are creating during the early days will be well worth the work you are putting in now, no matter how many messes you have to clean up along the way.

CHAPTER 5
Being a Puppy Parent

"Cavaliers love to be with you, so include them in whatever activities you are doing: gardening, walking, watering, or anything else."

Robbie Slemaker
Mayfair Cavaliers

Whether you have raised a puppy before or are a first-time puppy parent, you will undoubtedly encounter unanticipated things. Every dog is different and comes with its own set of joys and troubles. This chapter will review many of the potential challenges you will encounter with your growing Cavalier and help you navigate through them with minimal stress.

Photo Courtesy of
Roxanne Fisher

Photo Courtesy of Julia Deighton

Have Realistic Expectations

The first thing you should remember before becoming a puppy parent is that it's not always fun. Having a puppy is hard work and takes a lot of time and dedication. Caring for a puppy involves getting up in the middle of the night to take your dog outside, going through an entire bottle of stain remover cleaning up accidents, and always keeping a watchful eye to be sure nothing is being destroyed by those sharp puppy teeth. No matter how well-mannered your particular puppy may seem, almost no puppy parents get by completely unscathed and many lose a forgotten pair or two of shoes along the way.

If you think raising your new Cavalier will be easy, you may want to reconsider. Puppies are challenging. As discussed previously, they take time, money, and patience to raise properly. The reward you will receive after going through the challenging phases together will be a well- mannered, properly trained, loyal, and loving Cavalier that will always stick by your side.

Chewing

One of the most frustrating things about caring for a puppy is the chewing. Chewing is a way for puppies to explore the world and also to relieve any pain caused by incoming adult teeth. It is inevitable and unstoppable so don't reprimand your puppy for doing what comes naturally. Instead, be sure your puppy has plenty of safe toys or rubber bones to chew on so he's not tempted instead by the leg of the coffee table.

If you catch your puppy chewing on something inappropriate, remove the item or the puppy from the situation and give him an appropriate chew toy. This positive "take and replace" technique is far preferable to and much more effective than yelling at or punishing the puppy. Never let your puppy chew on your fingers or hands. This is a habit that is very difficult to break once established.

If your puppy is a persistent chewer, you may want to invest in some bitter-apple spray. This is intended to deter dogs from chewing due to its bad taste.

Chewing due to teething will most likely stop when all adult teeth have come in, around five to six months of age. However, some dogs chew more than others and will continue the habit into young adulthood. In these cases, it is important to always have a safe and desirable chew toy available to your Cavalier.

*Photo Courtesy of
Jade Bromley*

Photo Courtesy of
Maaike Palstra

Digging

Dogs dig for many reasons. Some dogs dig out of boredom, some because they're hot and want to lie in the cool dirt, and some just for the fun
and adventure of it. Because Cavaliers are primarily indoor dogs, digging is
not typically an issue with the breed. However, if you do have a spunky Cavalier that loves to get his paws into the dirt, you may need to take some precautions around the yard to keep your plants, lawn, and dog safe.

If your Cavalier is trying to dig under a fence, you should first try to find
the reason he may be doing this. Is there another dog on the other side of
the fence? Are there typically people on the other side he may be trying to
befriend? If this is the case, consider asking the neighbor if you can set up
a meeting between your dog and the people or animal he wants to get to
know. It may curb his desire to dig under the fence if he knows he can access his new friend another way. Follow all usual precautions for new dog
or people introductions to protect the safety of all parties.

If this doesn't stop the problem, or if your dog just seems to be digging
holes in the yard or garden for the fun of it, you may need to take a different approach. Try letting your Cavalier outside under supervised conditions
only. Allow your dog to do his business and then offer him a game of fetch.
If you allow your digging Cavalier to entertain himself, you may just find a
few more annuals dug up in your yard.

Barking and Growling

"When a Cavalier puppy finds his voice for the first time, he will do some barking. He will bark at anything that looks strange, especially his shadow."

Evelyn Knowles
Koncerto Cavaliers

Photo Courtesy of
Emma Jones

A well-bred Cavalier is almost never aggressive by nature. If you're in the middle of a tug-of-war match with your new puppy and you hear him let out a vicious growl, you may be concerned. Take heart, though, because a puppy is usually not growling out of aggression. When puppies play, they will often display loud barking, growling, chasing, and even pouncing. This is natural in a puppy's development and is exactly how they would be playing with their litter mates to establish new skills and better coordination.

If you want to discourage play fighting, don't do it by punishing your puppy. These are natural behaviors that should simply be ignored. If your puppy begins to play too rough and bark and growl, stop playing immediately and walk away. Come back to play when the puppy settles down. If your puppy continues to play too rough when you return, repeat the process until your puppy grasps the idea of what is and is not acceptable. This will take time but is well worth the effort.

If your dog seems truly agitated or begins snipping and biting in a way that seems defensive, it may be time to schedule a trip to see the vet. Truly agitated growling and biting behavior in a previously well-mannered dog can indicate a health problem that may be causing your dog pain.

Separation Anxiety

"Cavaliers can suffer from separation anxiety - you need to be home most of the time to own a Cavalier and keep them happy. They do not do well if left along more than a few hours at a time, but if you have another Cavalier or dog that helps alleviate their anxiety tremendously."

Judy
Laurel Crown Cavaliers

Most puppies will whine or bark when left alone. This is normal behavior and will typically stop as the dog becomes accustomed to short spans of time alone. However, a dog with separation anxiety will bark and pace persistently until you return. He may become destructive, chewing and clawing things out of distress. Even a housetrained dog may urinate or defecate in the house repeatedly when left alone if he suffers from separation anxiety. In extreme cases, a dog may display signs of coprophagy, a condition when a dog defecates and then consumes the stool.

The cause of separation anxiety is unknown and can occur in any dog. Because Cavaliers need so much attention and companionship, they may be more likely than other dogs to display separation anxiety when left alone for too long. Treating separation anxiety takes patience and understanding. Dogs are pack animals and instinctually do not like to be alone. The anxiety they feel stems from a very real and primal fear of being abandoned.

It may be helpful to take your dog for a walk or play fetch with him for a while just before you leave. Hopefully, this will tire your dog out and he will be too exhausted to get worked up while you're gone. You can also try leaving your dog with an interactive toy. Try a treat ball or a dog puzzle that will reward him with treats periodically. This may be just enough distraction to get your dog through his time alone. Make this toy or puzzle a special thing your dog only gets when he's alone. This can help positively reinforce that being alone can be a treat.

If the separation anxiety is severe and nothing seems to work, make an appointment with your vet to check that there is nothing else going on. They may be able to advise you on some safe ways to keep your dog calm when you have to leave the house.

Crate Training Basics

Dogs are not true den animals by nature, but they need a safe, quiet space to go to when they feel scared or anxious. In the wild, dogs and wolves only den when they rear puppies. These dens are usually holes dug in the ground by the mother wolf. The holes are abandoned when the puppies are old enough to travel with the pack. Although domesticated dogs' ancestors didn't spend their days in a den, that doesn't mean your new puppy won't find comfort in a "den" of his own in your house.

Crate training is a controversial topic among dog owners. Some believe the crate is a cage and inhumane. Others believe the crate is a necessary tool used to protect and secure a dog. The fact is, crate training your Cavalier makes puppy ownership more convenient for you and safer for your puppy. When done properly, crating your dog is an excellent tool for house-training and will set your dog up for success from the start.

When shopping for a crate, there are multiple types to choose from. These include plastic crates, wire crates, soft crates, and heavy-duty crates. The two main types are plastic and wire. If you plan to travel with your dog by plane, you will need to purchase a plastic crate as these are the only crates allowed for air travel.

Another common type of crate is the wire crate. These crates allow more visibility and airflow. They also fold flat for easy storage when not in use. These crates, depending on the size, often come with a removable divider. This is an excellent tool to use when potty-training your new puppy as it keeps the space small, so your puppy doesn't soil one end. You can line your crate with a commercial crate pad or an old towel or blanket for comfort. Regardless of what type of crate you buy, be sure you get one big enough for your dog when he is fully grown or else you may end up having to buy another one.

HELPFUL TIP
Travel

Your Cavalier is a small dog, 13-18 pounds on average, and generally easy to travel with. To provide a pleasant and safe trip, your dog should be placed in a special harness or carrier. Bigger is not better when it comes to pet carriers. At about one-foot tall, your pet's carrier should allow him to stand up, turn around, and lie flat. Carriers should allow for good ventilation, be top loading, and be made of sturdy material.

The key to crate training is positive reinforcement. The crate is intended to be a safe haven for your dog, a place he can go for rest and comfort. Do not ever put your dog in the crate as

Photo Courtesy of
Dina Baričić

a form of punishment. This sends the message that the crate is a bad place and will create issues going forward. You don't want your dog to view the crate as a "timeout" box or he will never retreat there willingly.

The first time you introduce your new puppy to the crate, you'll want to have some training treats on hand. Secure the door of the crate to the side so it doesn't accidentally swing closed and scare your puppy. Begin by placing a treat or two outside, near the door of the crate. Depending on how your Cavalier reacts to the crate, slowly place the treats closer until you can put one inside. Your puppy should voluntarily go inside the crate to get it.

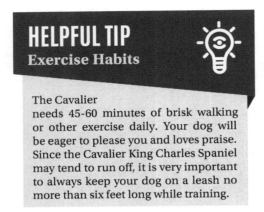

HELPFUL TIP

Exercise Habits

The Cavalier needs 45-60 minutes of brisk walking or other exercise daily. Your dog will be eager to please you and loves praise. Since the Cavalier King Charles Spaniel may tend to run off, it is very important to always keep your dog on a leash no more than six feet long while training.

Don't shut the door of the crate the first few times he goes in. Instead, praise him and allow him to come in and out of the crate freely. After your puppy becomes comfortable with the open crate, guide him in there and gently latch the door. Give him treats from the outside crate and verbally praise him. This will help him feel comfortable. Practice this exercise the first day you get your puppy home to get him fully comfortable with the crate before his first night in it.

Any time you need to crate your dog, do so by rewarding him with treats and a special toy. Praise him and make it a fun experience to get inside the crate. Don't leave your dog in the crate for long the first few times, with the exception of nighttime, or he may begin to get anxious and associate those feelings with the crate. Practice leaving your puppy in the crate while you're home for short increments of time, thirty minutes to an hour. Always immediately take your dog outside to his potty area when you let him out of the crate.

Be sure to exercise your dog thoroughly before expecting him to have any crate time. It is not reasonable for you to put your dog in a crate without first allowing him to expend his energy. Doing this will allow him to rest and sleep in his crate while you're away, further minimizing the chances of separation anxiety.

The crate is a tool that should be used responsibly. Never leave your dog in a crate for an extended period of time or treat the crate like a dog-sitter. Hopefully, with proper training, your puppy will outgrow his need for the crate and will no longer need to be confined to it while you're sleeping or away. Until then, always use the crate with care. If your puppy doesn't view the crate as a place of rest and comfort, you may need to reevaluate the way you're using it.

Leaving Your Dog Home Alone

The first time you leave your Cavalier home alone can be nerve-wracking for both of you. Hopefully you have already introduced your dog to the crate and allowed him to practice spending time alone in it. Before leaving your dog for the first time, play with your dog vigorously to wear him out or take him on a jog or a long walk. When it's time for him to go into the crate, follow same guidelines in the previous section. Reward your dog with a treat for entering the crate and give him a special "crate only" toy as an additional reward and boredom buster. Interactive treat toys like Kong work great for this.

When you return from your first trip away, it may seem fitting to greet your puppy with an excited hello but refrain so you don't make your dog think getting out of the crate is more exciting than going in. Going in the crate should be fun and exciting but getting out should be no big deal. Open the door to the crate casually and without much fuss. Remember, the crate is a safe and secure place of rest for your Cavalier, not a place of punishment or a place of waiting. If you let your dog out of the crate with too much excitement, you will inadvertently train him to be hyper and overexcited when the crate door opens.

Crate training will take time and effort. Some dogs take to it quickly and easily while others need more time and practice. Your Cavalier naturally will not like to be left alone as they are highly social dogs that crave time with their owners. It is especially important that you don't overuse the crate with a Cavalier, causing him anxiety and loneliness. This can lead to social and behavior issues. If you intend to leave your dog home for an extended time while you work, you may want to look into dog daycare or reconsider the Cavalier as the right breed for you and look into a breed who requires less in the way of constant companionship.

CHAPTER 6
Potty Training Your Cavalier

Potty Training Methodology

Potty training your Cavalier puppy will take a lot of time and energy. It typically takes four to six months for a dog to be fully potty trained, sometimes longer. The only proper way to potty train is by using positive reinforcement. Gone are the days when people told you to reprimand a dog and "rub his nose in it." This method simply does not work and is a cruel punishment for a puppy that doesn't know any better.

The goal is to teach your new puppy that your home is also theirs. Instinctually, dogs will not soil the places where they eat and sleep. Slowly in-

Photo Courtesy of
Roxanne Fisher

Photo Courtesy of
Shanna Mixon

troduce your dog to small, controlled areas of your house until he views the space as his own. This could be in a puppy play pen or a wire crate in the room with you when you first start the training. Over time, you can expand the area your dog is allowed until eventually he knows that he should only relieve himself outside.

Take your puppy out often, about every hour, and reward him freely with verbal praise and treats. Try to consistently take him to the same area so he will smell his scent and know that it's time to potty. Make this time with your puppy calm and all about the business. Do your best to ignore his attempts to play until after he's finished so he doesn't forget the reason he went outside in the first place.

It may take ten to fifteen minutes, but when your dog relieves himself, celebrate enthusiastically and reward him with a treat. This will help show him that going potty outside is a positive and fun experience. Your Cavalier will want to please you so once he gets the notion that this is what makes you happy, he will be much easier to train.

Using the Crate for Potty Training

"Use a crate; it's a huge tool for proper potty training. Start with a small one. If the crate is too large, they will potty in one side and sleep in the other and that defeats the purpose."

Brooke N.
Painted Blessing's Cavaliers

The crate is a great tool to use for potty training because it allows you to control your puppy in a small space during the times you can't supervise him. If you're using a wire crate, install the divider inside so that the accessible area is big enough for your dog to comfortably stand and turn around in but not big enough that he can take several steps to the other side. This will prevent him from soiling one side and sleeping on the other.

If you're not sure how often you should take your new Cavalier outside, a good rule of thumb to follow for a young puppy is for every month old he is, that's how many hours he can wait to go potty. That doesn't mean that you should only take your puppy out that often, because if you do, you will most likely be cleaning up a lot of accidents. This is simply a guideline for how long a young puppy can be left in the crate before needing to go out. Never leave your puppy or dog in the crate longer than four to six hours except for at night when everyone is sleeping.

When you wake up in the morning, immediately take your dog outside to the designated potty area. It probably will not take him long but give him several minutes. If you're planning to put your dog back into the crate while you're gone for work, take the time to exercise him thoroughly before you do. This will help your dog rest better while you're gone. You will need to come home to let your dog out at lunch time. Follow the same procedure before putting him back into the crate.

If you can't get back home to take your dog out at lunch, you will need to make other arrangements. Doggy day care is a great option. They will help you continue the potty training process and also help with socialization. Usually these places require certain vaccinations so be sure to call and check ahead of time. If doggy daycare is not an option, call a friend or family member to come by and let your puppy out for you. You can even hire a dog walker to come and exercise your pup while you are away. Go through a reputable service like Care.com so you can read references and know they've had a background check.

If you absolutely have to leave your dog in the crate or a puppy-proofed room for longer than you should, you can use a puppy pad on one side of the crate. This will slow down the training process because you will, at some point, have to remove the pads and retrain your dog that the only acceptable place to go is outside. If you will be consistently leaving your dog in the crate for extended periods of time, you may need to consider the well-being of your dog and explore other options. Cavaliers love their people and will not be happy spending most of the day alone.

Charles Weidig of BlackFire Cavaliers gives some great advice for anyone choosing to use a crate in potty training:

Charles Weidig – BlackFire Cavaliers on Crate Training

Crate training, done properly, is the most effective housebreaking tool. Here is a brief summary of how to do it:

As soon as your puppy wakes up in the morning, approach the crate using the same words each time, such as, "Do you want to go out?" Carry him outside to the same area each time and stay with him until he eliminates.

Give him time to find the right spot, and don't distract him.

After he is finished, give him lavish and enthusiastic praise – perhaps even a small treat. Then bring him back inside for a short period of SUPERVISED play. This period should start at no more than 15 minutes the first few days, and very gradually be increased over the following few weeks.

At the end of the supervised play period, put him back in the crate.

For the first few weeks, do not keep your puppy in the crate for longer than 2 hours at a time during the day. After that time period, wake him up and repeat the above procedure.

You should also follow the "go out" procedure after every meal.

As he gets older, he will be able to tolerate up to 4 hours at a time in the crate.

By GRADUALLY extending the period of supervised play, your puppy will become less and less dependent on the crate to prevent accidents, and will eventually have free rein of the house when with you.

The First Few Weeks

"The dog will only succeed based off of your effort. Some Cavaliers train fast because the owners are diligent and others take longer when they aren't. I recommend taking them out to potty 20 minutes after you feed and water them, and then reward them with a small treat. Do not leave food and water constantly out for them while potty training."

Kacey Leitheiser
Kacey's Cavaliers

The first few weeks of training your Cavalier will be challenging. In the beginning, take your dog out every hour or so during his daytime awake hours. He may not need to go every time but give him ten to fifteen minutes to try. Even if you have a fenced backyard, it will benefit you to take your dog outside on a leash. This will allow you to control where he goes and help him not be too distracted. Don't forget to praise him verbally and with a treat as soon as he finishes. This is an important step in helping him realize this is what you want him to do.

Photo Courtesy of
Morgan Behrens

How to Handle Accidents

"Learn to recognize the behavior your Cavalier exhibits just before peeing or pooping. Watch closely when they are out of their kennel. When you see that behavior start, get them to the proper place to go potty. Then praise them for doing it and play with them. Never punish or spank your puppy."

Evelyn Knowles
Koncerto Cavaliers

Accidents are going to happen so go ahead and buy that odor-neutralizing cleaner! Learning to potty outside is tough for a young puppy and requires patience by all. If you have been trying to train your dog to go on the grass, accidents on rugs and carpets are inevitable. The feeling of the carpet on a dog's paws is very similar to the feeling of grass and can sometimes trick a young puppy into thinking he can relieve himself there. If this becomes a problem, you might want to temporarily remove any rugs from your puppy's designated area until he gets the hang of going outside.

If you catch your dog in the act, quickly pick him up and take him outside to the potty area. Don't punish or yell at your dog. Most often, accidents are a direct result of the owner not taking the dog out enough. Sometimes a dog will soil a carpet just minutes after coming inside. Regardless, your puppy is still learning and should not be punished for the mistake. Punishing will only confuse your dog and prolong the potty training process.

Pros and Cons of Doggy Doors

Doggy doors can be beneficial in your effort to potty train, especially for older dogs. If you have a secured backyard, a doggy door can allow your dog to let himself out as he pleases. This could mean fewer accidents and a shorter training period. You should never let your dog go outside unsupervised unless you know the backyard is completely secure and your dog can't escape. Adding a doggy door is not for everyone, though, and you should review this list of pros and cons before making your decision.

Installation: Installing a doggy door is making a permanent change to your home and they are notoriously difficult to install. If you don't own your home, a doggy door is probably not an option for you.

Unwanted Visitors: Doggy doors are great for allowing your dog to freely come in and out of your home, but they may unintentionally offer that same freedom to unwanted wild animals as well. Luckily a Cavalier won't need a large doggy door so it probably won't be a way for thieves to get in, but it could definitely be an entry point for a much smaller masked bandit, like a raccoon!

Indoor Cats: If you have an indoor cat, it will be nearly impossible to keep him from leaving through the doggy door. If your cat has been de-clawed, this is particularly dangerous because your cat will have no defense from predators. If you have an indoor cat who already loves to go outside, a doggy door will allow him to bring his "treasures" inside the house. Finding a dead snake or bird in the house is probably not what the doggy door was meant for.

Securing the Yard: Before allowing your dog unsupervised time in the yard, you must be sure it's a safe area. Be sure the fence is secure and add a lock to any gate so neighborhood kids or thieves cannot let your dog out. If your dog is a digger then you may have a problem with him digging out to go explore. This is dangerous because he may encounter predators or cars on his big adventure outside the yard.

Photo Courtesy of Cindy Insley

Backyard Pool: Another danger to consider in the backyard is a pool. Even if your dog enjoys swimming, he should never be allowed near the pool unless you are out there with him. Swimming alone is dangerous, even for a dog. Allowing full access to the house and pool also permits your dog to come in and out freely while sopping wet, causing a big mess for you to clean up when you get home.

Fire Escape: One positive to a doggy door is it allows your dog to escape the house in case of an emergency. This could potentially save your dog's life in the event of a fire.

If you know your yard is safe and secure and you want to install a doggy door to aid in training, go ahead! You will still need to confine your dog's indoor privileges to a small space while still allowing access to the doggy door. This can be done by using a play pen set up against the wall.

A doggy door is not always a good option, but in the right scenario it can be very helpful. For elderly or disabled owners who have a more difficult time getting around, a doggy door allows the dog to relieve himself in the proper area without any burden to the owner.

Photo Courtesy of Melissa Parcell

If you decide on a doggy door, be prepared for a little bit of training; your puppy will not know how to use it otherwise. The first time you teach him to use it, give him a gentle push through, and have another person on the other side ready with a small treat and plenty of praise. Do this several times, in both directions. Once your puppy allows you to push him through without resistance, go to the opposite side of the doggy door, extend your hand through to the puppy, and allow him to smell the treat in your hand. Use the treat to lure him through. The third and final step is to call him from the other side, and give a treat when he goes through by himself. If you spend 5 or 10 minutes a day doing this, your Cavalier should be going through by himself within a week.

CHAPTER 7
Socializing Your Cavalier

"The Cavalier King Charles spaniel is a love sponge, one that gets along with everyone and everything. They are always happy, always upbeat and happy to be alive and with their family. Their faces are unforgettable, their expressions are sublime, their mannerisms are like no other, when you see a Cavalier, you just smile."

Enrique and Val Hinojosa
Cavaliers By Val

Photo Courtesy of
Kari Puzzullo

Photo Courtesy of Sophie MacGill

Importance of Socialization

"Enroll in puppy classes as soon as your vet gives you the 'go ahead' that their vaccinations will properly protect them. The most critical imprinting time when your puppy will soak up socializing easiest is between 2 & 4 months of age and continues through the first year. Don't lose this important time to socialize as it becomes much harder if you wait to start when they're older."

Brooke N.
Painted Blessing's Cavaliers

Cavaliers are naturally social, showing love and affection toward people and dogs of all sizes. However, without proper socialization, your dog may not fully come into his loving potential. By beginning your dog's socialization early, you can be sure that he will be able to coexist with any people or dogs he encounters in any environment. This will make life easier for you if you take your dog for walks at the park, restaurants, or other crowded outdoor events.

Behavior Around Other Dogs

Imagine a world where people greeted each other the way dogs do by sniffing, circling, and jumping up and down playfully. That would be quite a silly sight! Luckily for us, we humans have strict social guidelines to follow when we encounter each other. Dogs also have a set of social rules, but they are not nearly as strict as ours.

Much like people, dogs greet each other differently at a first meeting than they greet an old friend and much of it depends on the individual dog's personality. Dogs typically greet each other in one or all of the following ways:

Sniffing: Probably the most notable and joked about canine ritual is the sniff test. When dogs greet one another, they may begin with the muzzle or go straight for the backside. Sometimes the sniff will be brief and sometimes it can seem like a full- blown investigation. Unless one dog seems uncomfortable, this is perfectly normal behavior and doesn't need to be stopped. Once the dogs have satisfied their sniffers, they can move on to the next step in the canine greeting.

*Photo Courtesy of
Gayle Seale*

Play Stance: Have you ever seen a dog approach another dog and immediately go into a play bow? This behavior is simply one dog attempting to initiate play with another. It's like he's saying "Hey there! Do you want to be friends and play together?" Even a quick playful growl accompanied by a friendly tail wag is acceptable. Again, as long as neither dog seems stressed, there is no need to stop this behavior. Even if the other dog declines the offer to play, that doesn't mean the meeting was not successful.

Exerting Dominance: This particular greeting is probably the least endearing but is still acceptable in the canine world. One dog may exert his dominance by being the first to sniff and by non-aggressively showing the other dog he is in charge. This could include mounting. This process may be obvious to you or it may all happen so quickly that you don't even notice until little Sparky rolls over to show his belly in submission. As with the other behaviors, these are the natural social ways of dogs and should not be stopped unless there is real aggression or stress. Dogs take social cues well and are pretty good at keeping each other in line. If one is displeased, he will probably let the other know pretty quickly.

Safe Ways to Socialize

"Wait till all immunization shots have been given, and then I recommend finding a puppy kindergarten class at a training facility near you. They are naturally a social butterfly but it's great to get them used to different breeds of all sizes."

Kacey Leitheiser
Kacey's Cavaliers

The way dogs behave around each other can vary from breed to breed and dog to dog. If you're bringing your Cavalier home as a puppy, socializing him with other dogs should be easy. In general, puppies are more adaptable and willing to meet other dogs. Socialization should begin as early as possible, but be sure not to allow your puppy to have close contact with dogs you don't know until he has had his complete series of puppy shots.

If you choose to socialize your puppy with a leash on, keep your puppy close on leash or on the other side of a barrier, such as a gate, when you make introductions with other dogs, especially those that are older or larg-

Photo Courtesy of
Clare Talbot

er. Preferably all other dogs should also be leashed or somehow restrained in case anything goes wrong.

Allow the dogs to greet each other for a few seconds and then walk away. Each owner should distract their dog at this point until they are no longer interested in the other dog. If the initial interaction went well, allow the dogs to come together again in the same manner. Keep the leash loose so the dog can maneuver but not so loose it becomes a tangled mess. Read each dog's body language to determine how the greeting is going. Bodies should be relaxed and there should be no staring contests. As the dogs become comfortable and relaxed with each other, you will be able to let them off leash and they can have supervised play.

Some trainers believe first-time dog greetings should always be done off-leash so that the dogs are allowed to behave and greet each other more naturally. They believe that some dogs will feel trapped by the leash and become more defensive in nature, making the greeting unnatural and awkward. If this is the method you choose, make sure the owners of both dogs are fully compliant and willing to meet in a safe and neutral fenced area.

A first-time greeting should never be done in one of the dogs' yards. This could be seen as an invasion of territory for some dogs and cause a defensive reaction. Allow the dogs to meet but monitor their body language. If they use the body language described above, you don't need to interfere. But if either dog seems stiff, uncomfortable, or agitated, separate the dogs and use distractions to get their attention off of each other. Off-leash greetings can bring a greater risk if you don't know the other dog well and should only be done with friendly, pre-socialized dogs. Safety is the most important thing when socializing your dog so only do what you feel comfortable with.

Socializing Adult Dogs

If you're bringing an adult Cavalier into your home, the socialization process may take some extra time and careful planning. Depending on the dog's previous situation, he may not be used to other dogs. Oftentimes with a rescue, you don't know exactly what his life has held up until the point he was rescued. He may have been kept in a cage his whole life, abused by his owner, or even previously attacked by a bigger dog. All of these things are unknowns that could have a significant impact on his social abilities.

Be patient with your dog, no matter his age, and allow him to socialize on his terms. If your dog seems to have trouble socializing, take it slow and avoid putting your dog in situations that will cause him stress. This will only cause setbacks.

When dealing with an unsocialized adult dog, begin slowly at home. Take your dog on a walk around your neighborhood where he can see other dogs indirectly. He should eventually become comfortable enough to walk by other dogs in their backyards or on leashes without becoming stressed.

When he has successfully mastered these indirect encounters, it's time to move on to the next step.

If you have a neighbor with a dog, this is a great place to start direct socialization. These dogs will probably encounter each other at one point or another and will benefit by getting to know each other. Ask your neighbor and arrange a time to allow both dogs to meet, on leash, in a neutral part of the yard. Take things slow and give them space if either seems stressed. Follow the three-second rule and then walk away and distract each dog. Allow the dogs to come together again if the first encounter went well. If it doesn't seem to be going well, that's okay! Allow the dogs to just be in the yard at the same time until they become used to each other and then gradually allow them to interact more as it seems appropriate.

Keep your demeanor calm and stress free so that your dog doesn't pick up on any tension. It's all about establishing trust between you and your dog and between your dog and your neighbor's dog. Speak to your neighbor and his dog in a friendly and confident tone to help show your Cavalier that they're not a threat. With enough positive interactions, your dog should eventually warm up to them and become more social.

If you don't have a neighboring dog, call a friend with a dog or take your dog to a dog park. A dog park can be overwhelming depending on how many dogs are there so this may be a last resort as a place to socialize. Begin by just walking around the perimeter at a comfortable distance. Listen to your dog and take his cues. If he seems comfortable, allow him to interact more closely with a dog through the fence. If he remains calm, praise him. Reward him for positive encounters and remove him from negative ones. Try to only let him interact with dogs that are also calm. It will not help the situation to engage with a loud, barking, rambunctious dog through the fence. This could cause stress for an unsocialized dog and stop progress.

Another great option for socializing your Cavalier to other dogs is to enroll in a beginning obedience class at a local training center. This should only be done after he has had his full series of puppy shots, and is beginning to mature. Arrive at least 10-15 minutes before the class begins, and sit quietly with your dog (on his lead), so that he can get accustomed to the environment, and begin to feel confident in the presence of other dogs. Once the class begins, he will be focused on learning to do some basics of obedience, while surrounded by other dogs. You will also learn how to teach him valuable commands, like heel, sit, stay, and come, which will come in very handy throughout his life.

*Photo Courtesy of
Anna Balen*

Meeting New People

Introducing a Cavalier puppy to new people should be easy. Remember, puppies are generally easygoing and take to new friends well. This is especially true for a Cavalier pup. The main thing you will want to teach your puppy about meeting new people is not to jump. This can be challenging because when your puppy is small the jumping may seem cute. However, once the dog grows, the jumping becomes a problem and it's much harder to correct the behavior if it was once allowed.

Ideally, when approached by a person, your puppy should have a minimal reaction. He should remain calm but happy and keep all four paws on the ground. If you need to stop a jumping habit, begin by teaching your dog an alternate command. "Sit" is a good command to combat jumping because your dog can't do both at the same time. When your dog gets overly excited and begins to jump, counter by giving the "sit" command. Reward him for sitting and staying calm. If he can't stay calm and continues to jump, leave the room and ignore your dog for thirty seconds to one minute. Return and try again. This process works well for meeting new people, getting the leash out for walks, or any other exciting event that gets your dog jumping.

Introducing a rescue dog to new people can be a different story. Not knowing your dog's past means not knowing if he's had any negative human interactions. Begin any new introductions with people much like you would with dogs, slow and controlled. If your rescue Cavalier is a bit socially stunted, you probably had to work to gain his trust. Apply those same principles to anyone you want to introduce to your dog.

If you're having guests over, ask those people ahead of time to remain calm and not show the dog much attention. This may help ease your dog's mind and keep him calm. If your guests want to rub and love all over him, even with the best intentions, it could cause him to become overexcited and stressed. Once calm and comfortable, the dog may be trusting enough to allow a belly rub or two, but it should always be on his own terms. Give your guests some training treats to gain his trust. If your dog is particularly shy and nervous and you don't see much progress being made, try separating him with a baby gate so that he can observe the people but not feel pressured or overwhelmed.

Don't be afraid to take your Cavalier out into other situations where he can meet people. One of the best places for this is in your local big-box home improvement store. Most of them not only allow dogs, but welcome them warmly. It's hard to make your way from the electrical department to the lumber area without a dozen or so friendly people asking to say hello and pet your Cavalier! Have a few small treats handy, and ask people to give one to your puppy – he will quickly learn that meeting people is a good experience.

With enough patience and diligence, almost any dog can become well-socialized. A well-bred Cavalier should make the process easy, but it's still important to follow the guidelines above for the safety of your own dog and others.

Cavaliers and Children

Because of their lack of aggression, Cavaliers are trustworthy and gentle with even the littlest of children. Quite often Cavaliers and their children become best friends, often bonding over games of fetch or tug of war.

The breed is small and delicate but also very tolerant so remember to always teach your children to be gentle and kind, never pulling ears, hair, or tail. Show them by example the

HELPFUL TIP
Families With Children

Your Cavalier will need socializing early on during training. If you have children, encourage them to sit on the floor while interacting with the new dog. Doing this may discourage jumping activity while training. Cavaliers will bond with smaller and larger dogs but should be introduced slowly to other pets and animals to avoid aggression.

proper way to pet and hold your Cavalier so that they understand how to safely handle him. No matter how friendly and trustworthy your Cavalier is, never leave a child and dog alone unattended. This is for the safety of both the child and the dog.

CHAPTER 8
Cavaliers and Your Other Pets

Interspecies Introductions

Descended from the spaniel, the Cavalier possesses a natural hunting instinct. It's not powerful enough to drive the dog, but it will make him more apt to chase small animals and other objects. It's probably best to keep small animals like birds, rodents, and rabbits away from your Cavalier if they don't need to interact. If you have a pet of another species that you want to interact with your Cavalier, begin the introductions as young as possible and with constant supervision.

To introduce your new Cavalier puppy to a resident cat, begin without the animals by exchanging their scents. Keeping the animals separated, place a blanket or toy with the puppy's scent near the cat. Do the same for the puppy in a different area of the house. Let the dog and the cat sniff and become accustomed to the scents before a face-to-face interaction.

After exchanging scents, allow your pets to indirectly interact. Keep them separated by a gate or the crate but allow them to view each other. Depending on their reactions, you may feel comfortable enough to let them loose but be careful – your Cavalier puppy probably can't do much damage to your cat, but your cat can definitely harm your puppy if he feels threatened. Try introductions with someone gently holding each animal. Let the two sniff and explore but watch carefully for claws. Praise both animals for calm and reasonable reactions. Stop the introduction immediately if there is any fear or aggression shown.

Most likely, your Cavalier pup will just want to make friends with your cat and play right away. Your cat, on the other hand, probably won't know how to handle all of this playful affection and will need a place to escape. This escape should be off the ground in an area where your dog can't reach.

*Photo Courtesy of
Kelly Symons*

Introducing an Older Dog

You will need to take a different approach to introducing an adult Cavalier to a resident cat. An adult dog can cause real harm to a cat and the cat can do the same. Begin with the scent exchange described above.

After a day of getting accustomed to the other's scent, allow the two to meet through a closed door. Depending on personality, either pet may not be very interested in the other or they may be busting down the door to see who that is on the other side. Allow each animal to become calm and relaxed before any face-to-face interactions.

Once the two have become relaxed and calm on both sides of the door, allow the two to meet with the dog on a loose leash. Allow them a brief interaction before separating them and distracting to divert their attention. If the initial interaction was calm and peaceful, try again. If you decide to let the two interact with your dog off-leash, always allow your cat to escape to his safe space, designated just for him.

Friendship may not blossom overnight, but time will likely ease any tension. Cats and dogs can live peacefully together and can even form close bonds, but it probably won't happen overnight. With enough patience, your Cavalier and cat will be best buds in no time.

Photo Courtesy of Janet Scorgie

Aggression/Bad Behavior

The Cavalier King Charles Spaniel almost never has issues with aggression. However, despite a reputable breeder and good genes, improper treatment can ignite aggression in almost any dog. Animal abuse can cause deep-seated issues for your Cavalier that manifest as growling, snapping, or biting at you or other pets. This is especially important to remember if you're bringing home an adult rescue dog with an unknown past.

If your Cavalier does display aggressive behaviors, first take your dog to the vet to be sure there is no underlying condition causing him pain. Once this is ruled out it's time to evaluate the dog's current situation. Is there anything causing your Cavalier unnecessary stress? Is he being left alone too long? Is he being given enough attention and exercise? A Cavalier demands a high level of attention and affection and his behavior could suffer from not getting it.

If your Cavalier is showing aggression toward other dogs, begin by taking the proper steps to socialize him. Take it slowly and don't progress to direct interactions until your dog can keep his cool consistently. For dogs dealing with aggression issues, this could take much longer to achieve.

If your dog is showing aggression toward other pets at home, first begin by identifying the source. Is it food aggression? Does your Cavalier become possessive over toys or treats? If you identify the source, remove it. If your dog is dealing with food aggression, eliminate the situation by feeding your Cavalier in another room, away from all other pets. If he is particularly possessive of a favorite toy, only allow him to have the toy in the confines of his crate or designated alone area. Removing your dog from the stressful situations will not solve the aggression problem but it will make life easier while you deal with the root cause.

As long as your dog isn't causing any physical harm to you or any other members of your family, continue to work on carefully socializing the dog, rewarding friendly behavior with treats and praise. If the aggression doesn't improve or evolves to physical harm in any way, seek a professional trainer's help immediately. Never leave a potentially aggressive dog alone with another animal or unfamiliar person.

Photo Courtesy of
Linda Connelly

Rough Play or Aggression?

Many dogs growl and bare their teeth when they play. This does not automatically mean your dog has aggression issues. In fact, sometimes it can be quite difficult to distinguish between play and aggression.

When your dog and another dog are playfully bowing and taking turns chasing, rolling over, and mouthing each other, these are all signs that they are engaging in play together. Allowing this play to continue offers your dog great practice with social skills and is a wonderful outlet for excess energy.

FUN FACT
Breed Popularity

The Cavalier King Charles Spaniel is in the top 20 most popular dog breeds, according to the American Kennel Club (2018). Some famous Cavalier owners are Seth Rogan, Tom Selleck, President Ronald Reagan, Diane Sawyer, Ethel Kennedy, and Frank Sinatra. Tina Sinatra has stated she placed a small dog bone in her father's coffin because of his love of dogs.

If the dogs are playing but one or both seem stiff and tense, there may be more than a playful romp going on between them. Deep, drawn out growling, staring into the other dog's eyes, and a one-sided chase may all be indications that one or both of the dogs are showing some real aggression and you may want to end the encounter.

If you're having trouble with your puppy or adult dog playing too rough with you, the best thing to do is ignore him. In a pack of dogs, older dogs will naturally teach the younger pups when enough is enough. They do this by verbal cue and then ending play immediately. Even puppies of the same litter do this to each other. As the owner, you can take the same stance. When play becomes too rough, yip loudly and then walk away, ignoring your dog. After a minute, once the dog seems to have shifted his attention, return to play. Repeat this process until the puppy understands the rough play is not acceptable. Eventually he will understand the reason you keep walking away and will lessen his intensity.

Be aware of how you approach your dog for play. If you come in swinging and throwing your hands and arms around, this is encouraging your dog to play rough. Use toys instead of your body and keep movements gentle.

Photo Courtesy of
Susanna Collier

Raising Multiple Puppies from the Same Litter

There are many reasons why some people consider bringing home two puppies at once. They may believe that the dogs need each other to keep them company while they're at work. They may want to get a puppy for each child. They may even decide to get two because they just can't pick between them! While these may seem like valid reasons at first glance, you may want to reconsider.

Most experts warn against getting two puppies at the same time, especially from the same litter. You may think the work will not be that much more with one additional puppy but that's just not true. Each puppy will need to be crated, played with, and trained separately. There will be twice the mess and accidents to clean up, too. The work of caring for one puppy is hard but the work of caring for two puppies can easily be overwhelming.

It is true that the puppies will most likely grow up to be best friends. However, this often happens at the expense of the dog-owner relationship. They will create an inseparable bond with which you cannot compete.

A reputable breeder should always advise against getting two at once. Most of them will actually refuse to sell multiples unless you have proof that you can care for them both in a proper way. If you really want to have two dogs, get them at different times. Start with one so you can establish a bond and then if you want another, repeat the bonding process with that one before the two are allowed to pair up.

CHAPTER 9
Exercising Your Cavalier

"Cavaliers not only require exercise like any other breed, but they enjoy active interactions with their human partners. Exercise helps fend off heart disease, and strengthens the canine-human relationship. Anything from fetching a ball in the back yard to Agility competition gives a great opportunity for short bursts of fast activity. Long walks on a lead allow for prolonged, moderate cardiovascular exercise."

Charles Weidig
BlackFire Cavaliers

Exercise Requirements

Photo Courtesy of Gayle Seale

All dog breeds need regular exercise to keep them in good shape. Cavaliers may not be best suited to be intense running partners or swimming buddies, but if you're used to an active lifestyle and are looking for a way to get your Cavalier involved, try some agility training! Cavaliers' strong desire to please makes them a breeze to train and their small size makes it easier for them to master agility courses.

Cavaliers don't need an extremely active lifestyle to thrive. A minimum of a quick walk around the block once a day is all they need to keep them happy and in shape. As long as he is near you, your Cavalier will adapt and be happy with varying ranges of exercise.

86

Photo Courtesy of
Deb Hastings

How to Make Exercise Fun

If you're not interested in training your Cavalier in agility, there are other ways to make exercising your dog fun and exciting. Sometimes walking the same block or route in the park can become mundane, but walking your Cavalier is not the only way to get your dog's heart pumping. Try some of the following ideas to help you and your dog get past an exercise slump.

Use a Flirt Pole – A flirt pole is basically a stick with a toy attached to the end with a string. It allows you to engage your dog in a game of chase without much movement of your own. You can even use the flirt pole from a seated position. Because of Cavaliers' natural drive to chase, a flirt pole is the perfect solution for owners who are elderly or have limited mobility and cannot run alongside their dog. The flirt pole engages your dog mentally and physically, a win-win!

Play Hide and Seek – Once your dog has mastered basic commands and can sit and stay, try engaging him in a game of hide and seek. Take your dog to a chosen location in the house and have him sit and stay where he is. Your job is to go hide elsewhere in the house and then call him when you are ready.

HELPFUL TIP
Exercising Your Cavalier

Chasing games, such as tag and fetch, will help keep your Cavalier within a healthy weight range. These playful companions tend to gain weight easily and can develop bad habits if not thoroughly exercised. To avoid bad manners such as destructive chewing, jumping, and digging, provide your dog with enough physical and mental stimulation.

If your dog won't stay still long enough to allow you to hide, try giving him a treat that will take him half a minute or so to finish. Once he finishes, call to him from your hiding place and see how long it takes him to find you. Keep giving him encouragement until he figures out where you are. The game is fun for you and him alike and is a great way to give him exercise on a rainy day!

Play Fetch – So simple, yet so effective! There is not much a dog loves more than a game of fetch. Play with a tennis ball, rope, or Frisbee. Mix it up to keep things interesting. Teach your dog to return the item to your lap and this game can be a consistently easy outlet for excess energy.

Scavenger Hunt – A typical dog has up to 300 million olfactory receptors in his nose and the part of a dog's brain devoted to smell is proportionally 40 times larger than a human's. That means your Cavalier has a powerful sniffer! Make mealtime or snack time fun by creating a game out of it and putting that nose to work.

Hide small amounts of food or treats around areas of a room and see if your dog can sniff them out. If you hide them in enough areas, he may find himself running around the room from spot to spot trying to find the sources of the smell. While this may not provide as much exercise as one of the previous suggestions, it is still a way to get a lazy dog motivated on a dreary day.

Dog Day Care – Even if you spend most of your time home with your dog, an occasional trip to a local dog day care is a great way to give your pup some play time with other dogs while also allowing you to run errands without leaving your Cavalier alone. After a few hours at day care, your Cavalier will probably be exhausted and ready for a relaxing nap at home.

Importance of Mental Exercise

Although physical exercise usually gets all the attention, mental stimulation for your Cavalier is equally as important. A bored dog is often a destructive dog, especially with an emotionally needy dog like the Cavalier.

Tips for Keeping Your Cavalier Occupied

Many of the suggestions above serve as mental exercise as well as physical. Playing hide and seek, doing scavenger hunts, and using a flirt pole all provide a high amount of direct mental stimulation, as does interacting with other dogs at dog day care.

Another way to mentally stimulate your Cavalier is by teaching him a new trick. Cavaliers love to please and will enjoy training sessions. Learning a new command will help to further build the relationship and trust between you two, resulting in a generally more obedient and willing dog. After he has mastered all of the basic commands, get creative and teach your Cavalier some fun tricks like jumping through a hoop, walking backward, or crawling. You can even teach him to retrieve his toys by name and put them back up in their designated places.

There are toys and puzzles designed specifically with mental stimulation in mind. Kong makes a range of toys that can keep your dog occupied for a long time and are basically indestructible. A favorite is the "Classic Dog Toy." This is a rubber toy with a hollow center made for stuffing with treats.

*Photo Courtesy of
Joanna Loomes*

Kong has a safe line of treats and snacks or you can simply fill the toy with peanut butter. The Kong is dishwasher safe and costs between $8 and $25, depending on size, making it a great, affordable option.

Another option is a dog puzzle. The Trixie Poker Box has four compartments all covered by a lid. Your dog must figure out how each lid can be removed to get the reward waiting inside. All four lids open differently so this will take some real focus and determination on your dog's part. Once your dog figures out the trick to opening all boxes, this puzzle may not present a challenge anymore and he may want to move onto something else, so keep it in your arsenal for when your dog must be left alone.

If you prefer a mentally stimulating toy without the use of treats, try getting your Cavalier an Outward Hound Hide A Squirrel Puzzle Dog Toy. It's a hollow, plush tree stump with holes around it. Inside there are three plush squirrels that squeak. Your dog will have tons of fun trying to pull the squirrels from the stump. This is a great option for a dog who may need to watch his weight but probably isn't a good idea for a vigorous chewer as the squirrels are plush and can be torn apart with enough effort.

There are also electronic devices that you can control from a mobile device. Clever Pet is a unique system that challenges your dog with sequences,

Photo Courtesy of
Sonja Tomic

memory games, and electronically re-leased treats or food when solved. This system comes with a light-up pad that shows different colors and patterns. Clever Pet is designed to progressive-ly get more challenging as your dog fig-ures it out. Use the mobile application to track progress and monitor use. This system is wonderful for dogs who are left alone for long periods of the day. It comes at a $250 price tag but is worth it if it means you don't have to spend money cleaning up after a bored, de-structive dog.

Photo Courtesy of Jette Løfstedt

If your Cavalier loves a game of fetch, check out the iFetch Frenzy. Not as high-tech as the original iFetch, which is electronic and can launch a tennis ball up to 30 feet, the iFetch Frenzy uses gravity instead of electricity to drop the ball through one of three holes and send it rolling across the floor. As long as your Cavalier can learn to return the ball to the top, he can play solo fetch for hours while you are away.

If you find that your Cavalier has become particularly adept at perform-ing tricks, you might want to look into earning him a title as a Trick Dog. Both the AKC and the Cavalier King Charles Spaniel Club USA award Nov-ice, Intermediate, and Advanced Trick Dog titles. You will need to teach your Cavalier ten tricks from a prescribed list, and then go to a show where a judge will evaluate your dog's performance. If successful, you and your Cav-alier will both be rewarded for doing what is already a fun activity.

Rotate Toys

When you have to leave your Cavalier alone for a time, rotate interac-tive toys that will help to keep him entertained while you are away. Some owners even like to leave the television on while they're gone. There are specific shows on DogTV that are geared specifically toward dogs that some pooches really seem to enjoy!

CHAPTER 10
Training Your Cavalier King Charles Spaniel

"I personally find Cavalier King Charles Spaniels very smart and easy to train, especially since they are eager to please. This does need to be done with positive reinforcement."

Jenn Brisco
Cardinal Cavaliers

Photo Courtesy of
Sophie Lea Unsworth

Photo Courtesy of Sara Gregor

Benefits of Proper Training

Understanding your dog and knowing how to control him, develop his potentials, and resolve behavior problems, emotional conflicts and frustrations are no less essential than love and respect.

Michael W. Fox

Training your Cavalier will deepen the relationship between you and your dog, but it also serves an equally important purpose when it comes to safety. A properly trained Cavalier will come when called and will stay and obey out of trust and loyalty. This is particularly important in times of crisis or emergency. You should trust that your Cavalier will understand and obey in stressful situations. That obedience may even save his life.

As previously discussed, Cavaliers love to please their people. Your dog will want to obey and make you happy, he just needs to be taught how to do it. There are options when it comes to obedience training. You can search local advertisements and attend a group class, hire a personal trainer to come to your home, or train your dog yourself. No matter what you choose to do, be diligent and stick with the training schedule. The rewards of an obedient Cavalier will pay off for years to come.

Training Your Cavalier at Home

If you choose to handle the training by yourself or hire a personal trainer to come to your home, there are a few things you need to consider. Doing it yourself or hiring a trainer is a great way to fit training in to a busy schedule. If you can't make it to obedience classes regularly then a personal trainer may be the best option for you to keep things consistent. Training in your home can also keep your dog safe from any viruses that may possibly be lurking at a training facility that hosts many dogs a week.

One drawback, though, is not seeing how your dog reacts in less than optimal situations. There are many distractions for your Cavalier in a group obedience class but not so many in the quiet of your home. You need your dog to obey in any situation, at home or outside where there are potentially dangerous distractions everywhere. In a group class setting, your dog is learning to be obedient regardless of what is going on around him and this is an invaluable skill.

HELPFUL TIP
Training

Where would you like your new dog to relieve himself? Choose the area before you bring your puppy home. Start your dog's potty training prior to bringing him into the house for the first time. Do not change the spot. Puppies have small bladders and should be taken out frequently, every half hour or so. As your puppy reaches four months of age, this interval can be increased to every two hours. Praise your dog with words, not food, while potty training.

If you choose to train at home, occasionally take your dog somewhere else to practice obedience with real-life distractions. If you hire a trainer, ask them how they are making sure to train your dog in all situations and ask about the possibility of taking a training field trip to a public place. This option gives you the best of both worlds with flexibility while also ensuring proper training.

Maintaining Clear Expectations

No matter where you choose to begin obedience training, you should have clear expectations so you can be prepared for the amount of work it will take to successfully train your dog. You play as big a role in obedience training as your dog does, even if you don't choose to do the training yourself.

Obedience classes, either private or group, are usually held about once or twice a week. Most facilities require you to provide vaccination records before classes begin. Obedience training typically begins at about six months of age but dog ages in a class can vary widely. It

Photo Courtesy of Jacqui Wicks

is never too late to begin obedience training, so even if you have adopted a senior Cavalier, he's not too old to learn!

Before your first training session, ask for a list of materials you will need to bring. The facility will likely require your dog to have a leash and may ask you to provide your own training treats. Most obedience classes require a name tag with identification and some require a clicker. By purchasing all necessary supplies before class day, you can ensure that all your time is spent learning from the trainer and not scrambling to get what you need.

Even if classes are only held twice a week, be prepared to spend at least 15-20 minutes daily working on what your dog has learned. Just as with any skill, obedience training takes practice and repetition. It may not be easy, but this training will reinforce to your dog the idea that you are his pack leader.

Basic Commands

Obedience training is not just about learning to sit or shake. It is about building a trust between you and your Cavalier and communicating your wishes in a way your dog can understand. In order to build this trust, though, you must begin by teaching your dog basic commands.

Most obedience classes or personal trainers will begin the training by teaching a few easy, basic commands. These commands lay the foundation for more complicated tricks later. If you are choosing to tackle the job of trainer yourself, follow the steps below to master these five basic commands.

Sit – The sit command is the easiest one to teach and can be learned in a short period of time. Take your dog to a calm area free of distractions like toys. Have a bag full of very small training treats ready. With your dog

Photo Courtesy of
Anna Roberts

standing, facing you, hold a treat in front of his nose and slowly raise it up and over his head so he is forced to sit down and look up. Give the verbal command "sit" as you do this. When he sits, reward him with a treat and a key phrase such as "yes" or "good." If you're training with a clicker, also give a click when he obeys the command.

HELPFUL TIP
Your Dog's Vocabulary

When training your dog to respect your commands, use consistent verbiage. All family members should use language that your dog can depend on. You will want to teach the basic commands first, such as: quiet, sit, drop, come, and down. As your dog grows and learns these basic commands, you can extend your dog's vocabulary to include more difficult directions.

Down – Once your dog has mastered the sit command, move on to the down command. Guide your dog into a seated position, facing you. Hold a treat in front of his nose, lower it to the floor, and give the verbal command "down." If your dog raises his backside to a standing position to retrieve the treat, take the treat away and say "no." Begin again from a seated position. When your dog successfully lies down to retrieve the treat, reward with a treat, a positive verbal cue such as "yes," and a click.

Heel – Teaching your dog to heel requires him to walk on your left side at your pace whenever you're out and about. The heel command is a bit challenging and requires significant focus from your dog. He must stop when you stop and walk when you walk, never stepping in front of your left heel. This command is great for preventing leash tugging.

Begin by having your dog sit in front, facing you. Using your left hand, let your dog smell the treat and then swing your arm around to the left, luring your dog to turn around and stop in a position next to you but slightly behind, facing the same direction you are. Reward your dog immediately when he arrives in the correct position. Use the command "heel." Repeat this command many times, always having your dog come to the heel position before rewarding him.

After your dog has mastered the heel position, progress by taking a few steps using the same verbal "heel" command. Reward your dog for walking with you in the correct position. If your dog leaves the correct heel position, guide him back to where he is supposed to be before continuing.

Stay – To teach your dog to stay, command him to sit, facing you. With a visible treat in hand, hold up your palm to your dog and say "stay." Take one step backward. If your dog doesn't move, quickly return to your dog and reward him. You don't want your dog leaving the stay position to retrieve the treat. If your dog moves, say "no" and return him to a sitting position. As your dog gets the hang of "stay," increase the number of steps.

Leave It – This command is valuable and can help keep your dog safe if he gets into something potentially dangerous. Begin with two treats, one in each hand. Keep one hand in a fist but allow your dog to sniff the treat. As your dog tries to get into your hand to get the treat, verbally command him to "leave it." Repeat this command until your dog backs off and then reward with the treat from the other hand. As your dog progresses, make the treat more accessible and challenge your pup to leave it in exchange for another treat.

Training Methods

There are two main methods when it comes to training a dog: alpha dog training and positive reinforcement. Hotly debated among dog trainers, these two methods are vastly different. When choosing the method that is right for your dog, you must take some things into consideration and understand the details of each one.

Alpha Dog Training

Alpha training, popularized by television's dog trainer Cesar Millan, focuses on making yourself the alpha, or the leader of the pack. This training begins early by maintaining heavy control over your dog's actions. Users of this method are told to never allow your dog in your bed, not let a dog go through a doorway before you do, and never get down at eye level with your dog. It is also advised that you touch your dog's food to get your scent on it before giving it to him and don't let him eat until you give the verbal okay.

HELPFUL TIP
"Good Dog"

To discourage inappropriate behavior, be consistent with your Cavalier. Reprimand your dog firmly but gently when he is exhibiting unsuitable conduct. Pet owners should never use physical aggression to chastise their dogs. In order for you to gain the trust of your pet, treat him with respect and consistency.

Proponents of this method claim that dogs are pack animals and need to have a sense of who is alpha in order to learn to submit. They claim that wolves will assert their dominance over one another to keep each other in check and they attempt to achieve the same assertion by using highly controversial methods. In reality, research has shown that wolves in the wild actually do not have such a rigid hierarchy. They live socially among each other much like humans do with our own families. Also, cross-species dominance has not been proven successful at any point in history.

When it comes to obedience training, alpha training employs the use of restraints such as choke and shock collars and forceful body maneuvers. This method relies heavily on punishments and teaching your dog what he is doing wrong rather than teaching him how to do it right. While some trainers believe in the effectiveness of alpha training methods, others believe it is cruel and can actually undermine your relationship with your dog making it one based on fear and not trust.

Positive Reinforcement

"Cavaliers are eager to please their people, thus, they are easy to train. When you let the Cavalier know what you want it to do and reward the correct behavior, they learn fast. After a few repetitions, they should be trained. Cavaliers are also sensitive, so harsh or loud noise and hitting must be avoided."

Evelyn Knowles
Koncerto Cavaliers

The most recommended method of training today is positive reinforcement. The idea is that by reinforcing good behavior and obedience with desirable treats, your dog will learn the commands and build trust with the trainer. It is still important to let your dog know that you are in control, but this is done through positive reinforcement rather than force. Bad behavior is not punished by harm or discomfort, rather it is ignored or redirected until the positive behavior is consistent.

Dogs have been selectively bred over thousands of years to live alongside humans. Dogs, especially Cavaliers, thrive on companionship and will do anything to please their people. Using positive reinforcement is a method of teaching them to understand what you want them to do and teaching them that what makes you happy also makes them happy. This is the opposite of fear-based training and will build loyalty and trust naturally.

Primary Reinforcement

Primary reinforcements are directly related to innate, basic needs. These can vary depending on breed and animal but always include things such as food and water. Training treats are a primary reinforcement successfully used in training.

Secondary Reinforcement

Secondary reinforcements are things not based on instinctual, basic need but rather are cultural constructs. This includes verbal praise, smiles, and pats. Your dog must learn to associate these actions positively by pairing them with primary reinforcements.

Another type of secondary reinforcement is conditioned reinforcement. This is when something neutral, such as a whistle or a clicker, is used in conjunction with a primary reinforcement to create a positive association. Conditioned reinforcements can be highly effective initially but can lose their effectiveness when the primary reinforcement is taken away for an extended period of time.

Dangers of Correcting by Punishment

Correcting by punishment, as used in alpha training, has no scientific research backing it up as a legitimate training method. This type of forced control over a dog can lead to fear, anxiety, and can even put you or your family in danger. Using this method without an experienced professional's supervision can lead to a damaged relationship with your dog and a loss of trust.

Not only is this type of training risky, but it is also often ineffective. Your dog almost never does anything "bad" intentionally. He is aiming to please and if he is disobedient, it is most likely because he has not been taught what he is supposed to do. By punishing your dog when he does something undesirable, he will often be hurt and confused by what has happened. He may never fully understand which action was the reason for his discomfort in the first place.

Instead of punishing your dog to stop him from doing what he isn't supposed to, show him what he is supposed to do and reward him for that. It may take a little bit longer to master but your relationship will grow positively in the process.

In the early stages of training, you may have to gently guide your Cavalier into the desired behavior, and then give the treat. For example, in teaching him to come, you can have him on a lead, give the "come" command, pull gently on the lead to get him to approach you, and then treat when he does. The general rule for this is, "you do the work, and the dog gets the reward."

When to Hire a Trainer

If you are attempting to train at home but are having trouble making progress, it may be time to hire a professional trainer. Training a dog takes a lot of time and consistency and it is easy to get frustrated, sending your dog mixed messages while training. If the mixed signals go on for too long, it can actually cause major setbacks in your dog's progress. If you are dealing with any kind of aggression or poor social behaviors that do not seem to be improving with work, hire a trainer specialized in that area to help you get through to your dog. If you think you need help from a professional trainer, don't put it off. The sooner your dog is properly trained the sooner you can live together in peaceful companionship.

CHAPTER 11
Grooming Your Cavalier

Coat Basics

"Cavaliers shed often. Sometimes it is a few hairs, other times it is a lot of hair. Daily brushing helps with the shedding, but does not get all of it."

Evelyn Knowles
Koncerto Cavaliers

The Cavalier King Charles Spaniel's coat is as breathtaking as it is high maintenance. Cavaliers possess a top, silky flowing coat and a thin, shorter undercoat. Their silky top coats are long and feathered and can easily become tangled and matted. This chapter will take you through all the grooming basics you need to know to properly care for your Cavalier and his beautiful coat.

Basic Grooming Tools

The majority of your investment in grooming your Cavalier will be spent in time maintaining his coat. With just a basic set of brushes, scissors, and shampoo, you will have all you need to keep your Cavalier looking great. Since Cavaliers are typically not clipped, you will probably not need to invest in a pair of dog shears. Aside from coat care, you will also need to have nail trimmers, styptic powder, a dog toothbrush, toothpaste, and ear and eye wash.

Bathing and Brushing

"A simple daily or every other day brush works wonders, paying very special attention to where the bottom of the ear joins the head. The pads of their feet need to be kept clipped of hair as Cavaliers grow hair on their foot pads. That foot pad hair can mat and is very uncomfortable. A weekly check of the bottom of the feet with a clip is all that is needed."

Mark Fitchpatrick
Briarcliff Cavaliers

Regular brushing and baths are the key to keeping your Cavalier's coat looking clean and healthy. Brushing can happen as often as you like but is required at least on a weekly basis to prevent matting. Bathing, on the other hand, should only happen a maximum of once a month to prevent skin issues. Bathing your Cavalier too often will strip the oils from his skin and cause dryness.

When choosing a shampoo for your dog, look for one designated for a medium-coat type. Shampoo is largely chosen based on personal preference so you may have to try a few out before finding one that is just right for you and your Cavalier. Whichever shampoo you choose, make sure it is free from parabens, dyes, sulfates, and DEA. These are ingredients commonly used in commercial shampoos but are known to have potentially damaging effects over time. It is also best to avoid any added fragrances, especially if your dog has sensitive skin.

Finding a grooming brush for your Cavalier can easily become overwhelming because there are so many types of brushes all created for different purposes and coat types. Since Cavaliers are prone to tangles and mats, you will want to purchase a slicker brush. These are usually flat with short,

Photo Courtesy of
Raven Murray

fine wire bristles. The slicker brush is used for removing mats and tangles from the topcoat.

You will also want to purchase a natural bristle brush as a finishing brush. These brushes have tightly packed natural bristles and help to stimulate the skin's oils, keeping your Cavalier's coat shiny and healthy. Because the Cavalier's hair can grow so long between the pads of his feet, you will also need a good pair of hair cutting scissors.

Nail Trimming

Some people opt to have a groomer or a veterinarian trim their dog's nails but you can easily do this at home. You will need to invest in a quality nail trimmer. There are several types to choose from, but they will all get the job done so choose based on your preference and what is easiest for you to maneuver. You should also purchase some styptic powder. This will stop any bleeding if you accidentally cut a nail too short. Most clippers will come with instructions on how to clip the nails and it is important to follow them carefully to avoid injury to your dog.

Introduce the nail clippers to your Cavalier early and often. Let your dog explore and sniff the clippers so he can get familiar with them. Hold them down to his feet and show him that they are not a threat. Reward him with treats to create a positive association. Do this often, even when your Cavalier doesn't need a nail trim. This will help him to stay relaxed when it is time for an actual nail trimming session.

A dog's nail is made up of the nail and the quick. The quick is the pink part inside the nail. If your dogs has light-colored nails, the quick may be visible making it easier to avoid. If the nails are black you will not be able to see the quick and will need to be extra cautious not to trim too far back. If you do hit the quick, this is called quicking and is a very painful experience for your dog. It will bleed a lot so immediately apply styptic powder.

HELPFUL TIP
Shedding?

Cavalier King Charles Spaniels are considered heavy shedders. Weekly home grooming should take place two-three times per week, or, with professional grooming, every six-eight weeks. Owners will want to purchase a metal grooming comb, a grooming glove, and a pin brush to keep their Cavalier's coat luxurious and healthy. When you purchase a new grooming tool, introduce it to your pet before its use.

Photo Courtesy of Jenna Lovatt

Cleaning the Ears and Eyes

The long flowing ears of the Cavalier are a beautiful feature, but they don't allow much airflow into the ear canal. This makes them prone to infections. In order to prevent this, you need to clean your dog's ears out every week. To do this, gently squeeze one ear with cleaning solution as directed on the bottle. Massage the ear canal and then move on to the other ear. Unless your Cavalier is particularly cooperative, you will need someone to help you hold your dog while you put the liquid in his ear.

You will also want to regularly flush your Cavalier's eyes since they are prone to catching dirt and debris. Do this by using a dog eye wash and dropping the recommended number of drops directly into the eye. Consult the directions on the bottle to know how often you should flush your dog's eyes.

Dental Care

"Dental care is HUGE in this breed as they tend to have heart problems usually showing up half way through their lives. This can be greatly due to, or further aggravated by, the status of their dental health. Using a dental spray, brushing their teeth a couple times a week, and using a probiotic designed for oral health can often eliminate the need for dental cleanings all together."

Brooke N.
Painted Blessing's Cavaliers

Dental health is often overlooked when it comes to dogs but proper oral care is important! Dogs can suffer from the same oral diseases and pains that humans do. Your dog should be taken to the vet every year or two for a professional dental cleaning. Talk to your vet about how often he or she recommends.

At home, brush your dog's teeth with a dog-specific toothpaste often to prevent any oral issues down the road. Never use human toothpaste, which is full of additives that are meant to be spit out and not swallowed. Brush gently and take it slow until your dog is accustomed to the toothbrush. It is a good idea to do this at the same time you brush his coat every week to create a routine.

Bushing is not the only way to help your Cavalier keep his teeth in tip-top shape. Chewing has been shown to naturally reduce plaque and tartar build-up. Many dental chews are made for dogs of all sizes, and therefore may be a bit large for a Cavalier. When using these, it is advisable to have your dog on your lap and hold one end of the chew in your hand as he enjoys the chomping. This will ensure that your precious pup does not try to swallow a piece that is too big for him, and might cause choking.

To Clip or Not to Clip

"It is tempting to have a groomer shave down your Cavalier, but trimming destroys the flowing coat and natural look that characterizes the breed. If you trim, the only hair that should be cut is what pokes out from between the pads on the underside of the feet. Long ears and elegant feathering on the legs are to be treasured, and are worth the work of combing and brushing."

Charles Weidig
BlackFire Cavaliers

According to the American Kennel Club, the Cavalier's coat should never be clipped anywhere but on the bottom of the feet between the pads. If you aren't going to show your dog, you may find yourself considering a trim to help lower coat maintenance. Some even consider a shave during the summer months to keep cool.

Trimming and shaving your Cavalier is a bad idea if you like the silky texture of his coat. Oftentimes the hair that grows back is thicker, coarser, and curlier, a coat not desirable by breed standards. If your dog has to be shaved for medical reasons or because he finds himself in a sticky situation, literally, be sure to keep him protected from the elements. He will be susceptible to the sun, wet, and cold temperatures.

When to Seek Professional Help

It is very important to keep up with a regular grooming routine. If you find yourself too busy to get the weekly brushing or monthly bath done, consider hiring a professional. Do not ever neglect your Cavalier's grooming needs or you may find that it can get out of hand quickly and become a much bigger job.

If you don't want to see the groomer that regularly, consider hiring a local high school or college student. Pay him or her a weekly fee to come and brush your dog, clean the ears, and flush the eyes. As long as regular brushing is done, this should be a simple maintenance job. Just be sure you know and trust this person to do a proper job before you allow them to care for your Cavalier.

CHAPTER 12
Basic Health Care

Visiting the Vet

Aside from the first vet visit, discussed in chapter 4, your Cavalier should see the vet routinely for check-ups and vaccinations. At these regular visits your vet will give your Cavalier a good look-over to make sure things are still functioning properly. This should include listening to the heart and lungs and an examination of the ears, eyes, nose, and mouth. It should also involve an abdominal examination where your vet will feel for any abnormalities. He or she may also draw blood to check for heartworms and take a stool sample to check for other parasites. Sometimes the vet will examine your dog's gait and coat condition. Be ready to answer any questions he or she may have about diet or other routines for your Cavalier. Cavaliers can be susceptible to many genetic conditions so it is important to keep up with annual wellness checks with your vet so you can catch anything early before it becomes a bigger issue.

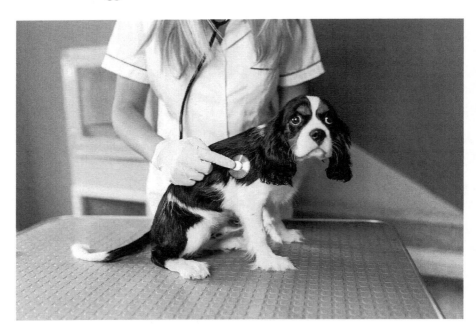

Photo Courtesy of
Emma Jones

Fleas and Ticks

Fleas are the most common external parasite to afflict dogs and they are a problem almost everywhere. They reproduce quickly and a single female flea can lay 20-40 eggs a day. If your Cavalier picks up a flea or two from the park and he has not been protected from fleas, you could be dealing with an infestation in your home before you know it.

Ticks can go largely unnoticed by their host, but they can cause a much bigger health problem than fleas. Ticks are notorious for transmitting dangerous diseases to dogs, humans, and other animals. While most ticks prefer your furry Cavalier as a host, they won't hesitate to latch on to you if they get the opportunity.

Flea and tick prevention is important for your Cavalier's health and for your own. There are many options when it comes to prevention and it is important you understand the benefits and the disadvantages of each one before you choose which is best for your dog.

One common way flea and tick preventative is administered is topically. Typically, this medication comes in a small tube that the owner squeezes onto the dog's back between the shoulder blades. This topical medication usually takes about 12 hours to take effect and will last about 30 days before it needs to be reapplied. This works because the solution is absorbed into

111

HELPFUL TIP
Health Concerns

Heart disease is the number one killer of Cavalier King Charles Spaniels. By age five, up to half of all Cavaliers will have heart disease. Other breed-specific diseases associated with Cavaliers are the neurological disorder syringomyelia, as well as hip dysplasia, eye diseases, food allergies, and skin conditions.

the skin and circulates through the dog's blood stream, treating fleas and ticks over the entire body, not just the area it was directly applied. One disadvantage of this application is it usually leaves a greasy spot on your dog's back for a few days. Considering this is a medication, it is probably not something you want to touch yourself or allow children to come in contact with.

It is important to note that topical treatments should never be used on a young puppy. In order to prevent adverse reactions, make sure to read the minimum age recommendations on the label, and consult with your vet before applying these.

Another method of administration is oral medication. There are numerous tablets on the market that prevent fleas and tick for 30 days. Some of these even prevent heartworms and internal parasites as well. Depending on how your dog takes medication, this could be an easier way to prevent the parasites without the mess of topical. Just as with any medications, side effects do exist. While they are generally mild, some dogs can react with skin irritations, vomiting, or diarrhea.

You can also buy a special flea collar for your dog. These are collars worn in addition to your dog's identification collar. They are covered topical flea medications, usually Permethrin. This provides long-lasting protection for your dog, up to eight months, but can cause skin irritation for your dog. While these collars have been deemed safe for dogs, permethrin can cause toxicity in cats. Just like with the topical medication, children and adults should avoid contact with the active ingredients on flea collars. As with topical medications, flea collars should never be used on a young puppy, and the same precautions should be taken with these.

Even if your Cavalier lives primarily inside, he should be on a flea and tick preventative. It only takes one exposure to one of these parasites to spell bad news for you and your dog. It is much better to take preventative measures than to have to deal with the fleas or ticks after they have hitched a ride into your home.

If your Cavalier scratches excessively and you suspect that he might have fleas, you can purchase a flea comb at any pet store. Flea combs have very fine and closely spaced teeth that fleas cannot pass between. Run the flea comb over your dog's body at a 45-degree angle, focusing on the areas where fleas are common (head, neck, hind quarters). If you see a flea caught up in the comb, cover it quickly with your finger and trap it in a wet paper towel. This will restrain, but not kill, the flea, so the paper towel will have to be disposed of outside the house.

You may also give your dog a flea bath. Vacuum your entire house from the floor to the curtains. Anything upholstered is potentially a place where a flea has laid eggs. If you notice fleas in your home, continue the vacuuming regimen twice a day for two weeks in order to get rid of all the fleas as they hatch.

If you find a tick on your dog, remove it immediately. Always wear gloves when removing a tick. Ticks carry serious diseases and you don't want to come into contact with their saliva or risk being bitten yourself. Once you have your gloves on, use a clean pair of tweezers and grab the tick firmly as close to the skin as possible. Pull firmly, straight up. You don't want to leave any of the mouth parts behind or this could lead to infection. Once you have removed the tick, place it in a jar of alcohol or soapy water. Keep the tick for identification in case your dog shows any symptoms of illness. Symptoms can take two weeks to surface so keep an eye out. Clean the bite thoroughly with antiseptic and watch the area for signs of irritation.

Photo Courtesy of Joyce Kearns

Vaccinations

Vaccinations prevent diseases by injecting the body with antigens to elicit an immune response producing antibodies for those diseases. The vaccinations cause no symptoms of disease but do give the body time to recognize and build up an immunity so that if the dog comes into contact with it, his immune system will respond fast enough to kill or shorten the illness significantly. Vaccinations are an important part in keeping your dog healthy and safe from potentially life-threatening illnesses.

A puppy will receive antibodies from its mother's milk for at least the first six weeks of its life and should be protected from many illnesses that way. Distemper, Adenovirus, Hepatitis, Parvovirus, and Parainfluenza are considered the core vaccinations that every puppy should receive at six weeks of age. These shots are usually given in four rounds: once at six weeks, ten weeks, fourteen weeks, and eighteen weeks. Most vets administer these core shots in a combination vaccine called a 5-Way. Depending on your area, some vets will recommend additional vaccinations. These may include Bordetella, Leptospirosis, and Coronavirus.

Photo Courtesy of Angel Page

Rabies is always administered separately and is recommended no earlier than 12 weeks. While some veterinarians may want to give it in addition to other combo vaccinations at your Cavalier's second-round appointment, Weidig strongly suggests no more than one vaccine be given in a single visit. "Multiple vaccines at one time increases the strain on the dog's immune system, and, if an adverse reaction occurs, will not allow the owner to identify which vaccine caused the reaction." Depending on where you live, legally your dog will have to receive a rabies vaccine every one to three years.

Reactions to these vaccines are rare but possible. Sometimes vaccinations can trigger an allergic reaction causing swelling, hives, vomiting, and fever. If your dog does have a reaction, notify your vet immediately. Even if the reaction is mild, make sure the vet is aware before your dog is given more vaccinations. The benefits of vaccinations far outweigh the risks. These vaccinations are one of the best ways to help set your dog up for a long, healthy life.

Common Diseases and Conditions

"There is a lot of controversy about the health concerns in Cavaliers. I have been a breeder for 15 years and have been very fortunate concerning health issues. I have had heart murmurs which Cavaliers will usually get as they get older and a lot of Cavaliers die of MVD (Mitral Valve Disease) in their old age. They can also get it at a young age, which is why you want to buy from a breeder who has health tested the parents. SM (Syringomyelia) is rapidly emerging as a severe inherited condition in Cavaliers. It is also knows as neck-scratching disease because a common sign is scratching in the area near the neck. It is a serious condition in which fluid-filled cavities develop within the spinal cord near the brain. I have only heard of a few cases of SM in all my years of breeding so I don't think it is as common in high quality health tested Cavaliers."

Judy
Laurel Crown Cavaliers

As lovable as they are, Cavaliers are also susceptible to a number of serious health conditions. The most notable of these is Mitral Valve Disease but there are a number of other illnesses that may affect your dog. Purchasing your Cavalier from a reputable breeder is one way to help protect against these diseases but it is not a guarantee. These diseases are prevalent even among reputable breeders. Almost none of these conditions are congenital, meaning they are not present at birth, so it is even more important to stay up to date on your dog's regular vet visits.

Mitral Valve Disease

Mitral valve disease is the most common ailment of the Cavalier and is the breed's leading cause of death. MVD is typically an old-age disease for other breeds but typically presents early and progresses more rapidly in Cavaliers. Nearly all Cavaliers will show some degree of MVD in their lifetime and it appears in over half of all Cavaliers by the age of five. Beginning with a heart murmur, mitral valve disorder is a degenerative disease causing the mitral valve to disfunction and can progress to heart failure within one to three years. Drugs may be used to manage MVD but there is no cure and eventually medications will no longer be helpful.

Patellar Luxation

Patellar Luxation is another inherited condition. It causes a defect of the knee allowing the patella (kneecap) to slip out of place. This condition can range in seriousness and may not even be noticeable at first. Depending on the severity, your vet may recommend surgery to manage pain and prevent further complications resulting from the patella being out of place. Some early symptoms of this disease are an unwillingness to place weight on a leg or a limp. Symptoms of a more advanced disease could be obvious discomfort and an unwillingness to walk.

Syringomyelia

Syringomyelia is a neurologic condition caused by Chiari-like malformation, which reduces the space for the brain, compressing and sometimes forcing it out into the spinal cord, causing a build-up of spinal fluid pressure as well as a number of symptoms including syrinxes, fluid-filled cavities of the spinal cord. Syringomyelia is rare among other breeds but it is thought more than half of Cavaliers possess this condition. Symptoms include head sensitivity and persistent scratching or shaking of the head and neck. Not every Cavalier with this condition will show symptoms. Syringomyelia is diagnosed with an MRI. Most affected Cavaliers will show evidence of this disease between six months and four years. Progression for these dogs is usually more severe than an afflicted dog showing no symptoms. Treatment for syringomyelia is typically pain management and prevention of further neurological complications.

Epilepsy

Various types of seizures are common for the breed but the most common is called "Fly Catcher's Syndrome." This causes a dog to appear to be biting at invisible flies in the air in front of his face. The exact cause or origin of this condition is unknown, though it is thought to possibly be a complication of syringomyelia.

Hip Dysplasia

Usually not diagnosed until two years of age, hip dysplasia is not a life-threatening disease but instead is one that can greatly reduce quality of a dog's life. Sometimes hip dysplasia can be managed with drugs, weight control, and monitored exercise. A Cavalier with severe hip dysplasia may need surgery to attempt to repair or replace the hip altogether.

Other Notable Diseases

Cavaliers are prone to eye complications including cataracts and retinal dysplasia. These conditions should be screened for by a certified ophthalmologist. Immune disorders are also possible including allergies, thyroid conditions, cancer, and other autoimmune disorders.

Holistic Alternatives and Supplements

"Cavaliers can have an issue emptying their anal glands; some people refer to it as the Cavalier Scoot! I actually give them a supplement to help them express their anal glands naturally. It's called 'Scoot Away' from Zesty Paws. But I do have a couple that still have to go the groomer or vet to get their anal glands expressed."

Kacey Leitheiser
Kacey's Cavaliers

If your pet has developed a hereditary condition, or if you want to take every precaution to prevent or delay one, the first step toward health and wellness for your Cavalier should be a healthy diet. Ensure your dog receives a quality diet. Dogs should have a high-protein diet limiting wheat, corn, or soy. Consider skipping the kibble and making your dog a homemade, nutrition-packed meal. Continue reading in the next chapter for more information on nutrition and dog food alternatives.

Acupuncture is becoming more common in pets because of its notable benefits in managing pain and increasing circulation. Supporting overall wellness, acupuncture can aid in the treatment of hip dysplasia, allergies, gastrointestinal problems, and pain due to cancer treatments. Acupuncture causes no pain for a small dog and is shown to have a calming effect. Acupuncture should only be performed by a certified acupuncturist and you should always consult your veterinarian before beginning any alternative treatments.

Herbs – Are a staple in holistic health care but not all herbs are safe for dogs and some can interact with drugs your dog may be taking. Discuss any herbs with your vet before adding them to your dog's diet or lifestyle. Some herbs include:

Goldenseal – Anti-inflammatory and anti-bacterial, goldenseal can be used externally on bodily infections or as an eye wash for infections or conjunctivitis. It can be taken internally at the first sign of kennel cough or digestive issues and can also be beneficial in the treatment of tapeworms and Giarida. Goldenseal should not be used for too long as it can cause stress on the liver.

Milk Thistle – Milk thistle provides liver support by protecting against damage. If your dog is on any medication that can damage his liver, discuss adding milk thistle to his regimen with your vet.

Ginger – Just as with people, ginger is an effective tool for treating nausea and even cardiovascular conditions in dogs. Ginger has cardiotonic effects and can promote functionality of the heart.

Chamomile – Another herb that helps aid digestion, relieve muscle spasms, and reduce inflammation. Chamomile is a great option for treating chronic bowel and gas disorders and can also ease your Cavalier's anxiety.

Licorice – Licorice root is a fast-acting anti-inflammatory that can be used for the treatment of arthritis and other inflammatory diseases. It has been shown to enhance the efficacy of other herbs, so it is often combined with others as a part of a treatment plan.

CBD Oil – As stated on the American Kennel Club website, "Currently, there has been no formal study on how CBD affects dogs. What scientists do know is that cannabinoids interact with the endocannabinoid receptors located in the central and peripheral nervous systems, which help maintain balance in the body and keep it in a normal healthy state."

CBD oil, also known as cannabidiol, is thought to treat pain and help control seizures in dogs. Anecdotal evidence also shows that CBD oil may have anti-inflammatory, anti-cancer, anti-anxiety, and cardiac benefits. Discuss with your vet the option of adding a CBD supplement to your Cavalier's lifestyle.

These are only a few of the herbs available for homeopathic use for your dog. If you want your dog to experience the benefits of herbal remedies but can't source the herbs yourself, there are many premade solutions and tinctures available for the holistic care of your Cavalier. They come conveniently packaged and mixed with directions so you can know you are using the herb correctly. Be sure to only use products from a reputable source that has a reputation for supplying the best holistic and herbal treatments. Beware of cheaper products that may contain synthetics.

Pet Insurance

Because Cavalier King Charles Spaniels are, on average, prone to more genetic conditions than most other breeds, it may be in your best interest to invest in pet insurance. It is advisable to carefully research each provider to weigh cost versus benefit before taking out a policy. Different companies offer different coverage so be sure to read the fine print and understand any exclusions. Talk with your vet to see if he has a company he recommends.

Rates will vary based on your dog's age, history, and condition. While it is generally considered more affordable to pay out of pocket for vet visits for common ailments, pet insurance can be a life-saver if something catastrophic arises and your Cavalier needs expensive tests, surgery, or medication for life.

CHAPTER 13
Nutrition

"Find out what kind of puppy food your breeder was feeding the puppy and continue on with that in the beginning. If you want to change their food you need to do it gradually by adding some of the new food in with the old."

Judy
Laurel Crown Cavaliers

Benefits of Quality Dog Food

Photo Courtesy of
Charlie Blankenship

When it comes to feeding ourselves, we know that there are some foods that are better for us than others. For the sake of our health, we do our best to eat a balanced diet and avoid processed foods with harmful additives. These same rules apply when it comes to feeding our dogs. Just like humans, dogs need a certain balance of protein, fats, carbohydrates, vitamins, and minerals to keep their bodies going.

All commercial dog foods have been tested rigorously and are required to meet minimum nutritional requirements. Although this is true, minimum requirements are not what is best for your dog's health long term. Feeding your dog low-quality dog food is the equivalent of feeding him processed junk food. Choosing a dog food that is made with the best ingredients and does not include preservatives and additives will help your dog function at his optimal level, including his immune system, potentially protecting against disease.

According to Dr. Hugh Stevenson, a veterinarian in Ontario, Canada, for over twenty years, poor nutrition can be noted by a dull, thin coat, poor-quality foot pads (which can crack or bleed), weight problems, excess stool and gas, and passing undigested grain particles in feces. Quality dog nutrition leads to a lustrous coat, healthy skin and weight, and less stool due to more of the food being digestible. When it comes to your lovable Cavalier companion, a quality food will give him the best possible start from puppyhood on.

Types of Commercial Dog Foods

"Cavs can be 'iffy' eaters, in other words, they don't know IF they're going to eat now or later or not even today, just to make their puppy parents crazy."

Enrique and Val Hinojosa
Cavaliers By Val

There are many dog foods that claim to be the best, healthiest, and most complete. It can be both overwhelming and confusing. Should you buy dry kibble? Canned wet food? Each contains a different list of ingredients and promises on the label so how do you really know what you're getting?

The first choice you will have to make is whether to feed your Cavalier dry kibble or wet food. Each choice comes with its own set of positives and negatives that may affect your choice.

Wet Dog Food: Wet dog food has a very strong smell. This may be a positive for a dog who is particularly picky or doesn't have much interest in eating as the strong scent may entice him to eat. It could also be a negative if you don't want to smell the food in your home every time you feed your Cavalier. Wet food also helps with hydration if you have a dog that doesn't drink as much as he should, but it spoils quickly after opening. If your dog doesn't finish his food promptly, you'll need to store the rest in the refrigerator. Canned food can also be a bit messier to eat, depending on your dog.

Dry Dog Food: Dry dog food is easier to store once opened because it doesn't spoil when left out. This is beneficial for a dog who may like to come back to his food and finish later. Dry dog food also doesn't have much of a smell so it can sit out in your home without anyone noticing. Some dry kibble has been formulated to help clean your dog's teeth while he chews although some experts say the added grains in certain dry foods contribute to tooth decay. If you choose to use dry food, make sure your Cavalier has ready access to water throughout the day, since the food does not provide any hydration.

Whichever type of food you choose for your dog, it's important to remember that both canned food and kibble exists in low-quality forms. Low-quality brands include cheap fillers, artificial colors, flavors, and preservatives and should be avoided.

Ingredients to Avoid

It can be confusing reading the ingredient list on a dog food label. Companies that produce low-quality dog food use vague terms and scientific words to try and make you think the product contains quality, wholesome ingredients when it may not. Below is a list of key ingredients to avoid when searching for the best commercial dog food for your Cavalier.

BHA/ BHT

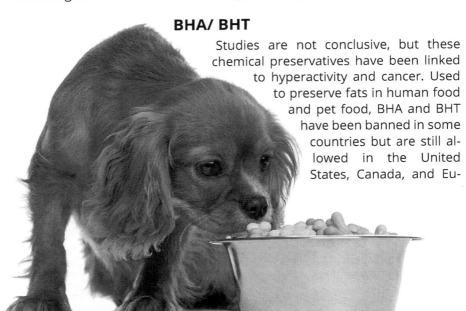

Studies are not conclusive, but these chemical preservatives have been linked to hyperactivity and cancer. Used to preserve fats in human food and pet food, BHA and BHT have been banned in some countries but are still allowed in the United States, Canada, and Europe. Until conclusive evidence proves these preservatives are safe, it's best to avoid them altogether.

Meat, Meat Meal, or Rendered Fat

Any time you see a vague, non-specific term such as "meat" or "meat meal," you can bet these are the lowest quality ingredients allowed. These ingredients are leftovers from slaughterhouses; the parts humans won't eat. It can also include leftover, expired meats from the grocery store and diseased and dying livestock. Instead, look for specific meat terms you recognize such as turkey, beef, salmon, lamb, or chicken.

If your dog food contains salmon or salmon meal, make sure it's labeled "wild caught." Farm-raised salmon is less nutrient dense than its wild counterpart because of the unnatural diet the fish are fed and has been found to potentially contain more contaminants.

Nitrites and Nitrates

Chemical additives used to preserve freshness and extend the shelf life of meat products, nitrates and nitrites are found in human and dog food. Sodium nitrite can be toxic to your dog in high doses and has been linked to cancer.

Soy

Soy is cheap and readily available. Dog food manufacturers may use it as an inexpensive way to boost the protein percentage of a food, but it can be difficult to digest for your dog and can cause gastrointestinal upset.

Other ingredients to avoid include meat by-products, sodium hexametaphosphate, food dyes, carrageenan, taurine, cellulose, artificial flavors and corn syrup. Dog food manufacturers dedicated to producing a quality, superior dog food will not contain these red flag ingredients. Though they can be a bit more expensive, the cost will be well worth it and may even save you money in vet bills in the long term by nourishing your Cavalier properly.

There has been a recent trend in grain-free dog food. We have demonized grains in our own diets and allowed the trend to carry over into our dog's bowls. Some claim that because wolves in the wild don't consume more than a trace amount of grains, domesticated dogs shouldn't either. The truth is, dogs are not genetically identical to wolves and they have adapted to effectively utilize gains.

In fact, grain-free dog food contains other plants instead of the grains. These are usually peas, lentils, potatoes, and legumes. These plant sourc-

*Photo Courtesy of
Zsoka Szabo*

es provide the starch to make the kibble as well as an added protein boost, allowing the manufacturer to cut back on the more expensive animal proteins. This can lead to a depletion of the amino acid taurine. Taurine is found in animal proteins but not in plant proteins and the FDA has linked this to a rise of cardiomyopathy in dogs who have been fed a grain-free diet. While the verdict is still out on grain-free dog food, it is best to discuss with your vet what food is best for your Cavalier before jumping on the grain-free trend.

Homemade Dog Food

Some owners choose to skip commercial dog food all together and make their dogs' meals themselves instead. This is the only real way to know exactly what your Cavalier is eating. If you have the time and resources, homemade dog food can provide your Cavalier with a wonderful source of balanced nutrition including real, whole foods and none of the preservatives found in commercial foods. In addition, food cooked at home contains more nutrients than processed food. This is because the high temperature used during processing causes significant loss of nutrients.

Many homemade dog food recipes can be found online but it's very important that you discuss specific recipes with your vet to be sure they provide your dog with all of the nutrients he needs. Individual breeds and even dogs of the same breed can have different nutritional needs. When making your dog's food yourself, it's important to get a professional opinion regarding ingredients and serving size.

Table Food

When it comes to feeding your dog table food, the key to safety is knowing what is beneficial and what is not. In Chapter 3 we already discussed a list of foods to never feed your Cavalier, so you may want to return there and refresh your memory before continuing on to this list of foods that are okay to share with your pup. Remember, feeding your dog directly from the table can quickly form bad habits such as begging. This may be cute the first time but may get old fast when you want to enjoy a meal in peace.

There are a number of things you can safely share with your dog from your kitchen as a special treat or snack, but remember that these should be given in moderation so they don't upset the balance of your dog's nutrition. None of these items should be heavily seasoned as this may cause an upset stomach.

- White and brown rice
- Cooked eggs
- Oatmeal
- Carrots
- Cheese
- Peanut butter (without xylitol)
- Berries
- Green beans
- Seedless watermelon
- Bananas
- Peas
- Pineapple
- Apples
- Broccoli
- Potatoes

This is not a comprehensive list and food sensitivities can differ from dog to dog so consult your veterinarian if you think your dog may have a food allergy or sensitivity.

Weight Management

There are two easy tests you can do to determine if your Cavalier is overweight:

1. Run your hand gently along the dog's side. You should feel the rib cage under a light layer of fat.

2. While your dog is standing, look at him from above. You should see a narrowing at the waist, just behind the rib cage.

If your Cavalier is overweight, you should deal with the problem immediately. Begin by implementing a more active routine. Consult chapter nine for ideas to make exercise fun for you and your Cavalier. Also consider where your dog is getting his nutrition. Is he eating a quality commercial food? Low-quality foods contain filler ingredients that will fill your dog up temporarily but don't provide adequate nutrients. Your dog may end up eating more of these foods to make up for the lack of nutrition, causing weight issues. If you prepare homemade dog food for your pup, you may need to go back to the vet or nutritionist to reevaluate ingredients and portion sizes.

Also consider what your dog is eating when it isn't mealtime. Are you sharing too many snacks from the kitchen with your Cavalier? Moderation is the key to sharing special treats and too many can be detrimental to your dog's health if it leads to obesity and disease. If weight is an issue for your

Cavalier, cut out the snacks all together and feed him only at designated mealtimes.

If you can't get your dog's weight under control by limiting snacks and providing a quality commercial food, discuss options with your vet. He or she may suggest a weight management food. These foods feature higher than average protein, lower than average fat, and fewer calories. These foods are formulated for adult dogs only and should never be given to a puppy. Remember to read food labels and choose a food made with high-quality ingredients.

HELPFUL TIP
Cavalier Nutrition

Good-quality protein should be the main ingredient in your Cavalier's diet. Included in the diet should be excellent sources of carbohydrates such as brown rice, oatmeal, sweet potatoes, or tapioca according to the National Research Council of the National Academies. Watch out for corn or wheat additives in your dog's food. These ingredients may cause allergies. If your dog develops allergies, purchase limited- ingredient dog food.

CHAPTER 14
Dealing with Unwanted Behaviors

"Cavaliers display unwanted behaviors from a lack of socialization, anxiety or ineffective training. If you are not able to modify or correct these behaviors then it is imperative to consult with the trainer."

Christine Vitolo
Royal Flush Cavaliers

What Is Considered Bad Behavior?

Dog personalities vary as much as human personalities. No two are alike. We all want a well- trained, obedient dog but even successful training won't keep a spunky dog from being spunky. Just like humans, dogs can exhibit behaviors that are annoying at times but that doesn't necessarily mean they are bad. So when it comes to bad habits and behaviors, what is actually considered "bad"?

FUN FACT
Dash and Queen Victoria

Queen Victoria of England loved her Cavalier King Charles Spaniel. When her beloved companion died, she commissioned a monument to Dash at his burial location at Adelaide Cottage, Windsor, Great Park.

Dash
"Here lies DASH, The favourite spaniel of Her Majesty Queen Victoria, In his 10th year, His attachment was without selfishness, His playfulness without malice, His fidelity without deceit, READER, If you would be beloved and die regretted, Profit by the example of DASH"

Barking: Barking is as natural for your dog as speaking is to you and should never be considered bad behavior. If your dog is particularly chatty and barks a bit too frequently, there are measures you can take to correct the annoyance. First, try to find the root cause of the barking. Is there a direct, consistent trigger such as seeing other people or dogs? If this is the case, socialization may be in order to give your dog a chance to engage with other pups and bark in an appropriate setting. If the problem is more sporadic and inconsistent, consider whether your Cavalier may simply be trying to get your attention. Are you spending enough one on one time with your Cavalier? These dogs have extremely high social needs and the barking issue may be a result of those needs not being met.

If your Cavalier still barks at inappropriate times, you might try a simple preventative measure. Take an empty aluminum beverage can, fill it with coins or nuts and bolts, and seal the top with tape. If the dog barks inappropriately (without a normal trigger), throw the can near him, and use a verbal prompt like "Quiet!" The noise made by the can will startle the dog, and he will come to associate the prompt word with the noise. Be sure to praise and comfort him when he stops barking. Of course, because this technique also relies on negative reinforcement, it should only be used sparingly and as a last resort.

Chasing – Some dogs, especially Cavaliers, are instinctually wired to chase things. This is what they were originally bred to do. While this behav-

Photo Courtesy of
Emma Jones

Photo Courtesy of
Tiffany Sumption

ior can become an issue, it should never be treated as "bad" behavior. Your Cavalier is only doing what comes naturally to him. Obedience training can help this issue but may not eliminate it completely.

Digging – Much like chasing, digging is a natural behavior and may involve rolling around the freshly disturbed dirt. This is not bad behavior but can become annoying and may be curbed with stricter supervision and obedience training.

Leash Pulling – This is a direct result of improper or inadequate training and is not bad behavior. Teach your dog the proper way to walk on a leash with the help of a trainer and this annoyance can be eliminated altogether.

Other unwanted behaviors that are not "bad" include chewing up toys or shoes that were left out, begging for or stealing food, jumping on people, getting on furniture, and eating poop. All of these behaviors can be a nuisance but are typically not evidence of a poorly behaved dog.

Aggression – Behavior that should always be considered "bad" is any form of unprovoked aggression. This could be vicious growling, biting, lunging, or snarling. These behaviors are unacceptable and if not dealt with immediately, can result in serious injury or death for your dog or the object of his aggression. This includes food or possession aggression. There may be a root issue or trigger that you are not aware of so consult a professional trainer or animal psychologist promptly if you are dealing with these truly bad and dangerous dog behaviors.

Finding the Root of the Problem

When dealing with any unwanted behavior, the first step to eliminating the issue is finding the root cause. Learning the why will make correcting the problem so much easier for both you and your dog.

Instinctual – If the unwanted behavior you are dealing with is something instinctually bred into your dog, it will probably be more difficult to correct. Try training with a professional but if that doesn't work you may have to redirect the unwanted behavior into an appropriate outlet. For example, if your dog loves to chase, find him a way to chase safely in a controlled environment. This applies to all instinctual issues including chewing and digging. Allow your dog to do these things in a way that is not a problem to prevent him from doing them in an inappropriate manner that may result in damaged or destroyed property.

Lack of Training – The majority of a dog's unwanted behaviors stem from a simple lack of training. Leash tugging, jumping, begging for food, and jumping on furniture are all a direct result of inconsistent boundaries set by the owner. Training your dog consistently and purposefully is the best way to correct these unwanted behaviors. See chapter ten for tips on where to get started.

If you are dealing with a true aggression issue with your dog, determine what the root cause might be. Could he be suffering from a health issue? Is there a traumatic event in your dog's past? A long-standing lack of socialization? If so, there may be a long road of recovery ahead for your Cavalier and you will more than likely require the assistance of a trainer and possibly a dog psychologist. These behavioral issues can be a matter of life or death for a dog so approach them with intention.

Photo Courtesy of
Danielle Scattergood

How to Properly Correct Your Dog

When it comes to correcting a dog, one thing is clear: punishment doesn't work. Unless your Cavalier has a deep-seated issue involving a traumatic past or mental condition, he will want to please you with his actions. Correct him by showing him what you want him to do instead of the unwanted behavior. If it's an issue that does not concern safety, do your best to meet your dog in the middle with a solution that will make you both happy. If he loves to chew, keep a steady supply of interesting chew toys at his disposal so that he can still chew but you don't have to worry about your belongings.

Photo Courtesy of Jenna Lovatt

When to Call a Professional

Sometimes, even seemingly harmless unwanted behaviors can become a dangerous issue for your dog. Digging can be harmless if it only leads to a few holes in the backyard, but if it evolves into digging under the fence, it can become a serious problem quickly, exposing your dog to the many dangers that lie outside the fence. Likewise, losing a few pairs of shoes to a chewer can be frustrating but not dangerous to your dog. However, if that chewer decides to eat a loose electrical cord or a toy with small batteries, it could end in an emergency trip to the animal hospital.

If your attempts to redirect your dog's behavior yourself have been futile, contact your local dog training facility and ask for help. They will undoubtedly have seen these issues before and will have the resources and tools to help you find a solution that works for you and your dog. It's important to seek help at the first sign of a problem and not let unwanted habits form. If you wait and habits do form, it will be much more challenging to correct the behavior down the road.

CHAPTER 15
Caring for Your Senior Cavalier

Caring for an aging dog can present a whole new set of challenges. Aging dogs, just like humans, typically require more medical care because they are prone to ailments such as arthritis, cognitive dysfunction, cataracts, hearing loss, incontinence, and inability to regulate body temperature.

Not all dogs reach this stage at the same time and many can live comfortable and happy lives for years, even with these ailments. This chapter will discuss potential issues you may face with your aging Cavalier and help you navigate the difficult end-of-life decisions when the time comes.

Common Old-Age Ailments

MVD – As previously discussed, nearly all Cavaliers will exhibit signs of mitral valve disease during their lifetime, typically evidenced by a heart murmur. This means that by the time your dog reaches the senior stage, more than likely he will have a heart murmur to some degree. This is not

*Photo Courtesy of
Janet Scorgie*

always a problem but should be monitored closely for deterioration by your vet, especially when your dog reaches senior age.

Arthritis – Osteoarthritis is a degenerative joint disease where the bones of a joint rub against each other due to the deterioration of the cartilage between them. This deterioration can cause severe pain, stiffness, and limited mobility. Osteoarthritis cannot be cured but can be treated with medication and supplements to slow the progression of the disease and treat symptoms.

Cataracts – Cataracts cause a dog to have blurry vision by creating an opacity

Photo Courtesy Of Anna Roberts

in the normally clear lens. If your senior dog develops cataracts, have your vet monitor him closely for worsening symptoms. When left untreated, cataracts can sometimes lead to blindness.

Cognitive Dysfunction – Senior dogs are susceptible to dementia just like humans are. If you notice your dog forgetting something he does often or acting unusually out of his normal routine, discuss options with your vet for helping improve his quality of life. If your Cavalier experiences these symptoms, try to ease his frustration and confusion by making everyday tasks simpler for him.

Hearing Loss – Hearing loss is common for old dogs. While many will lose some degree of hearing, they may not go completely deaf. Signs of hearing loss include a sudden lack of obedience, increased startle reaction, and excessive barking.

If your dog experiences hearing loss, you may need to find another form of communication. Teach your dog hand signals at the first sign of hearing loss so that if he loses his hearing completely, you can still communicate commands. It may also be helpful to keep a flashlight handy to signal for his attention.

Basic Senior Dog Care

When caring for your senior Cavalier, there are certain precautions you should take. Care for a senior dog should be focused on keeping him comfortable and happy. Like people, senior dogs have trouble regulating their body temperature. Be sure to provide your Cavalier with extra warmth on a cold day and make sure he stays cool on a hot day.

Special accommodations may need to be made to make life more comfortable for your senior dog. If your dog has arthritis, he may benefit from a specially made bed to help with stiffness. If you have stairs, you may also need to consider keeping all of your dog's things on the lowest level of your home so he doesn't need to climb the stairs.

As a dog ages, energy levels usually decline along with stamina. It's important that you give your aging Cavalier regular, gentle exercise to keep him in shape. Obesity can be a problem in older dogs who typically move around less, and it can exacerbate other age-related ailments such as arthritis and heart conditions. If obesity becomes a problem despite regular exercise, discuss options with your veterinarian. He or she may suggest switching to a different food.

Oftentimes, a dog's dental care is neglected throughout life leading to potentially painful issues in old age. If your elderly dog suddenly seems to lose his appetite, check with your vet to see if the problem could be dental. Sometimes a painful tooth or painful gums can be enough to deter a dog from his dinner.

Photo Courtesy of *Claire Findlay*

Your senior dog will probably need to see the vet more during his last years than he did previously. The AAHA (American Animal Hospital Association) recommends that you take your senior dog to the vet at least once every six months for a check-up. These regular vet visits can help you catch any conditions early and allow for more prompt treatment, potentially leading to a better quality of life for your Cavalier.

Illness and Injury Prevention

One of the most important aspects of senior dog care is preventing illness and injury. It's much more challenging for an elderly dog to overcome an illness or injury than it is for a younger dog.

As discussed above, exercise is just as important for a senior dog as it is for a young one. It should look a little different, though. Because a senior dog is more prone to injury, exercise should be done at a less vigorous pace that will have less impact on aging joints. Instead of going for a daily jog, take your Cavalier for a nice, slow walk or take him for a swim. Avoid activities that involve jumping or climbing an incline. These activities may risk injury or aggravation of arthritis, causing your dog unnecessary pain.

To protect your senior dog from illness, be sure to continue his parasite medication for fleas and ticks. Also, make sure he stays up to date on his vaccinations. If an elderly dog does fall ill, he is more likely to suffer complications that may be life threatening. A younger dog may contract the common Bordetella bacterium and suffer no real consequences but for a senior dog, a simple infection can quickly turn into pneumonia which may result in a hospital stay.

Supplements and Nutrition

Proper nutrition is more important than ever when a dog reaches his final years. Quality of life and severity of geriatric conditions can be greatly influenced by diet. There are many supplements on the market that are specifically formulated for senior dogs.

Before adding any supplement to your dog's diet, consult your veterinarian. He or she may be able to direct you to a quality brand or alert you to possible side effects or interactions with your dog's current medications.

Below is a list of the most common supplements.

Glucosamine and Chondroitin – Two supplements often paired together to combat osteoarthritis, glucosamine and chondroitin have been found to be therapeutic in the treatment of canine arthritis. These compounds are found naturally in cartilage and are made by the body.

When looking for a glucosamine and chondroitin supplement, look for highly reputable brands that source all of their ingredients from the United States. Imported glucosamine has been found to contain many contaminants including lead, especially when sourced from China. Since the FDA

HELPFUL TIP
Life Expectancy

Cavaliers have an average life expectancy of ten years of age. Owners should purchase dogs from responsible breeders who test their potential breeding stock for diseases commonly found in the breed. For a comprehensive list of recommended health tests, owners may check the website of the "Parent Club" of the American Cavalier King Charles Spaniels Club, Inc. (ackcsc.org) or the American Kennel Club website (cdn. akc.org).

does not regulate supplements, the only way to know if you are getting a quality product is to be vigilant and diligent in your research. Even popular pet store brands that say "made in the U.S.A." can include ingredients sourced from China.

Omega-3 Fatty Acids – Omega-3 fatty acids like DHA and EPA have been shown to be beneficial for a number of reasons that may benefit your senior dog. These fatty acids are beneficial for the brain, potentially improving cognitive function in old age and may even give his immune system a boost. According to the American Kennel Club, "The addition of omega-3 to the diet may [also] help reduce inflammation and can promote cell membrane health."

Antioxidants – Including an extra source of antioxidants in your senior dog's diet can be beneficial as well. You can do this by purchasing a supplement or by simply allowing your dog to snack on high antioxidant fruits such as berries and apples.

Probiotics – Probiotics help maintain healthy bacteria in the gut, the place where up to 80 percent of a dog's immune defenses reside. This can improve immune function and help your senior dog ward off illness and disease more efficiently.

When It's Time to Say Goodbye

Undoubtedly, the hardest part of being a pet owner is knowing when it's time to say goodbye. Our dogs devote the best years of their life to us, unconditionally gifting us with love and loyalty no matter the circumstances. When the time comes and you see that your beloved Cavalier is experiencing more pain than joy, it may be time to consider the most difficult decision you will face in pet ownership.

Many people believe that it is one of the toughest and greatest responsibilities of animal ownership to know when to humanely relieve an animal from the pain when the end of their life is inevitable. It is never an easy decision and often leads to an array of emotions for the owner including sorrow, guilt and second thoughts. These are normal and will probably never change no matter how many times you face this decision.

How will you know when the time is right?

No one knows your dog better than you do and no one will be able to make this decision for you. You and your Cavalier have a bond that nobody else can understand and that is exactly what makes you the right person to make the final call. If you have a gut feeling that your senior dog has made a sharp decline in health and is hurting more than he is enjoying life, it may be time to say goodbye. A few telltale signs that death is imminent are extreme lethargy, lack of interest in anything, loss of coordination, incontinence, and not eating or drinking.

Only you and your dog will know when this time is. Your dog has trusted you with his life during all the time you spent together and he trusts you with it now. If you believe putting him down humanely will end his suffering, speak to your vet and discuss euthanasia.

Once you have made the decision that the time has come to humanely end your dog's suffering, understand that second thoughts are normal. Don't second-guess the decision that is best for your dog just because it's hard for you. Grieving over this decision is natural and normal. Talk to a trusted friend or family member to help you cope during this difficult time.

Once you have made the decision, as long as the vet agrees death is inevitable, the process happens fairly quickly. The point is to end your dog's suffering so there is no sense in putting it off for a few days.

The Euthanasia Process

Before you take your dog to the vet, call any friends or family members who may want to say goodbye. You will have the option to be present when the vet performs the procedure. Although it may be hard for you to watch your dog die, know that it will bring your dog comfort and peace in his last moments if you are there with him, holding him and comforting him.

During the procedure, your vet will administer a solution, typically phenobarbital, intravenously. The solution is usually thick with a blue, pink, or purple tint. The vet may inject it directly into a vein or into an intravenous catheter. Once the solution is injected, it will quickly travel through your dog's body causing him to lose consciousness within just a few seconds. Your Cavalier will feel no pain. Breathing will slow and then stop altogether. Cardiac arrest will occur and cause death within thirty seconds of the injection.

Your vet will check for signs of life and will most likely step out of the room for a few moments to give you time to say a final goodbye. Your vet and his office staff have been through this before and will understand the emotional weight of the situation for you. They should provide you with privacy and be a source of comfort if needed. Be sure to make payments and after-death arrangements beforehand so you don't have to deal with it after.

Your dog's body may still move after death so don't be alarmed if you see twitching. He may also release bodily fluids and this is also normal. When you are ready, leave your dog and allow the vet to proceed with his remains. If you have chosen to have your dog cremated, your vet will coordinate with a cremation service and notify you when his ashes are ready. If you are taking your deceased dog home for burial, the vet will place your dog's remains in a container and will typically carry it out to the car for you. Whichever you choose, once you leave the vet's office you will begin the grieving process, remembering that the love and bond the two of you shared will always be in your memory.

Photo Courtesy of Samantha Foster

Golden Eyes

Carol Walker
Rainbowbridgeonline.com

When golden eyes no longer glow,
and we both know it's time to go,
Don't look at me with eyes so sad,
but think of better times we had,
When sunlight did upon us shine,
and happy days were yours and mine,
And through the grass we both did run,
and on our backs we felt the sun,
Think not of this dark final hour,
think not of when our lives turned sour,
Think not of hopelessness and pain,
but think of joy and laugh again,
For in that final act of love,
you released me to heaven above,
Where finally from pain I'm free,
where one day you will join with me,
Where together again we will rejoice,
and you and I as with one voice,
Will in perfect harmony sing,
of the joy and pain that love can bring,
And remember me just as I will,
always think of you until,
At last again I see your face,
grieve not, I am in a better place.

Made in the USA
Middletown, DE
25 September 2023

39366756R00080